LEARN PUNJABI

Sentence Structure Made Easy

team indic

team indic
www.teamindic.com

ISBN-10:0-9984828-0-3
ISBN-13:978-0-9984828-0-4

For orders and for other books by this author
please visit www.teamindic.com

Contents

INTRODUCTION

Our Goal

This course is a step by step guide for learning simple, clear and correct Punjabi. It is comprised of seven lessons which are designed specifically for English speaking people. No prior knowledge of the Punjabi language is necessary to benefit from this book.

A Unique Approach

This course approaches learning Punjabi from the standpoint of an English speaking background. Comparisons are made between English and Punjabi to explain concepts.

The main focus throughout the course is word order. It is vital for an English speaking person who wants to learn Punjabi to focus not only on pronunciation and vocabulary but also on learning how to arrange those new words into a sentence. To understand why word order is so vital, notice how confusing it is to see English words in the Punjabi word order:

"Every language in words random way in not arranged are."

The first lesson explains how to form a basic sentence and the following six lessons gradually explain how to build larger sentences.

Putting Theory into Practice

The course is laid out in a simple and logical manner. Each lesson builds on the previous lesson. We recommend starting on the first lesson and working your way through the entire course systematically. After completion of the course, the book can also serve as a reference guide.

Daily practice exercises are included with each lesson so that you can immediately apply what you are learning. The accompanying practice calendar is for tracking your progress for a month, so it is recommended to spend sufficient time practicing each lesson before moving on to the next lesson. Remember, the goal of this course is not simply to learn grammar but to start speaking Punjabi by putting theory into practice.

The Think and Speak Method

The daily practice exercises use the 'think and speak' method. Rather than writing out the answers, you will be asked to think about the answer and then say it out loud. It can be said that to learn to read, you need to practice reading. To learn to write, you need to practice writing. But to learn to speak, you need to practice speaking.

There is no answer sheet provided for the daily practice exercises. This encourages you to go back to the lesson and its accompanying charts for confirmation. The daily exercises can be done either individually or with a partner.

We recommend a daily practice sessions of approximately 15 minutes. Research has shown that brief but frequent practice sessions are far more beneficial than long but infrequent sessions.

Rotating Practice Schedule

Starting with lesson four, the practice calendar uses a rotating practice schedule. This means that practice sessions will rotate between the completed lessons, with the most recently completed lesson being practiced the most frequently. As you progress in the course, this method will aid you with long term retention. It has been observed, that as the length of time between practice sessions gradually increases, the strength of the memory increases. In effect, gradually reducing the frequency of practicing something will move it into your long term memory.

Learning the Punjabi (Gurmukhi) Script vs. Romanization

Due to popular demand, with this second edition, we have included Romanized text alongside the Punjabi script. We employed the standard method as cataloged in the US Library of Congress (https://www.loc.gov/catdir/cpso/roman.html).

Although this provides a means to get started quickly, we highly recommend taking the time to learn to read the Punjabi script. To assist you with this, follow this link to our website (http://howtolearnpunjabi.com/learn-punjabi-alphabet.php) to download a copy of Punjabi alphabet flashcards.

You will notice that each card includes image mnemonics. This means that each letter is associated with a picture that an English speaking person would be familiar with which approximates the sound of the letter. Each time you see the letter you recall the picture and thus can easily remember what the letter is. Using this method, it is not uncommon to learn the entire Punjabi alphabet in a few weeks. Doing so will aid greatly both with proper pronunciation and speaking the language fluently.

From Our Readers

"This course is amazing because I'm teaching Punjabi to primary students and I always face the problem of how I can teach sentence formation. When I teach my kids the way you explain in your lessons, they learn so easily. I'm so happy."
— Navjot, Canada

"The course fantastically analyzed the difference between the sentence structure in English and Punjabi which I have often struggled with."
— Hasdeep, United Kingdom

"The course organized everything I needed to know with regards to sentence structure in a manageable and easily understandable way. I wish I started here a year ago, who knows how much more Punjabi I could have learned."
— Vito, United States

"This course is very unique from the other courses I've seen and thanks to its simplicity, I can now write simple Punjabi sentences and even speak them. I'm very grateful! Thank you for making this gem for us who want to learn Punjabi."
— Yvonnie, Philippines

"I try to teach my children the Punjabi language but it is difficult teaching children who's first language is English. I like the way it is explained simply and broken down step by step, I feel more confident in teaching the language."
— Manjinder, United Kingdom

"I enjoyed learning through the systematic and simple approach. The emphasis on word order was a feature that I had never seen elsewhere and it was helpful."
— Raghbir, The United Kingdom

"I liked the way of teaching with fundamental and rich vocabulary and exercises."
— Ranjeet, India

"I love the way the comparison is made to the way English is taught."
— Jasminder, Indonesia

"It was concise and easy to follow and understand. Everything you needed was provided. The learner was kept in mind at all times."
— Ravinder, England

THE BASIC SENTENCE

Word Order (Syntax)

In every language, including English, the words in a sentence are not arranged randomly, rather, they follow a specific order.

When an English speaking person is learning Punjabi, they need to give special attention to the word order in Punjabi because it is different than the word order in English. Arranging words in the proper order is vital to being understood.

In English the word order is (subject + verb + object)

In Punjabi the word order is (subject + object + verb)

For example: "Nick sends letters" would become "Nick letters sends"

The subject, direct object and verb are the main parts of a sentence. These three parts of a sentence are like boxes. You can put one or more words into each box. To determine which box to put a word into, ask the following questions:

1. **What is being done? (VERB)**
2. **Who is doing it? (SUBJECT)**
3. **...what? (DIRECT OBJECT)**

SUBJECT	DIRECT OBJECT	VERB
Nick	letters	sends is
ਨਿਕ	ਚਿੱਠੀਆਂ	ਭੇਜਦਾ ਹੈ
Nik	*ciṭhṭhīān*	*bhejdā hai*

TIP: Always identify the verb first. If you start by identifying the VERB then you will never get your subject and object confused.

Putting Theory Into Practice

At this point, find page 19 entitled "Lesson One Worksheet." We will now practice rearranging English words into the Punjabi word order. This worksheet has five sentences for you to translate. Go ahead and follow steps 1 – 4 closely. We will do steps 5 and 6 later.

TIP: Punjabi does not use the words "a" or "the". So ignore these words when you translate into English.

Verb Endings (Inflection)

The next important matter to discuss is verb endings. In English, to a limited extent, the verb changes in order to match the subject. For example, let's look at the sentence: "Nick sends letters." If we want to say in English, "We send letters" then we would need to change "sends" to "send".

In Punjabi, a similar thing happens. The verb changes in order to match the subject. In Punjabi, the verb changes depending on whether the subject is:

1. singular or plural
2. masculine or feminine

How do we change the verb?

First: Find the stem (or root) of the verb. In Punjabi, this means simply removing the ਨਾ *nā* or ਣਾ *ṇā* ending.
For example: "to send" ਭੇਜਣਾ *bhejṇā* (the stem is ਭੇਜ *bhej*)

Second: Add the appropriate ending to the stem of the verb.
For example: ਭੇਜ *bhej* (stem) + ਦਾ *dā* (ending) = ਭੇਜਦਾ *bhejdā*

REMEMBER: The verb must match the subject. In our example sentence, "Nick" is a masculine singular subject, so we add the masculine singular ending ਦਾ *dā* to the stem.

In the present tense, there are four different verb endings:

masculine singular	ਦਾ *dā*	feminine singular	ਦੀ *dī*
masculine plural	ਦੇ *de*	feminine plural	ਦੀਆਂ *dīāṇ*

If you are using a pronoun (I, we, you, he, she, they) then use the corresponding ending from the "Present Tense Chart" on page 20. In this chart the verb root is shaded in gray and the verb endings are highlighted in red.

NOTE: The plural form of 'you' is used for respect and ALWAYS uses the masculine ending. The pronouns 'we' and 'they' most often use the masculine ending because even if only one in the group is masculine then the masculine ending should be used. Wherever possible, the chart shows the ending that is most commonly used.

Now, let's discuss the last column (highlighted in yellow) on the "Present Tense Chart" which is called "Aux. Verb".

The Auxiliary Verb "to be"

In English, we put a minimum of one verb into the verb box. However, in Punjabi, it is common to put TWO verbs into the verb box:

1. The main verb

2. The auxiliary verb

Most commonly, the verb "to be" is used as the auxiliary verb. In English, the verb "to be" can be expressed using the words: am, is & are. These words must match the subject. For example, singular subjects use 'is' and plural subjects use 'are.' If the subject is a pronoun, it has a matching pair.

For example: I <u>am</u> You <u>are</u> We <u>are</u> He/She <u>is</u> They <u>are</u>

In Punjabi, the verb ਹੋਣਾ *hoṇā* (to be) can be expressed using the words: ਹੈ *hai*, ਹਾਂ *hāṇ*, ਹੋ *ho* & ਹਨ *han*

1. Singular subjects use ਹੈ *hai*
2. Plural subjects use ਹਨ *han*

If the subject is a pronoun, it has a matching pair as shown below.

ਮੈਂ ਹਾਂ *maiṇ hāṇ*	ਤੁਸੀਂ ਹੋ *tusīṇ ho*	ਅਸੀਂ ਹਾਂ *āsīṇ hāṇ*	ਉਹ ਹੈ *uh hai*	ਉਹ ਹਨ *uh han*
I <u>am</u>	You <u>are</u>	We <u>are</u>	He/She <u>is</u>	They <u>are</u>

The auxiliary verb is put into the verb box after the main verb. Notice our example sentence one last time: "Nick sends letters" Nick is singular so we use the auxiliary verb ਹੈ *hai*

SUBJECT	DIRECT OBJECT	VERB + AUX.VERB
Nick	letters	sends is
ਨਿਕ	ਚਿੱਠੀਆਂ	ਭੇਜਦਾ ਹੈ
Nik	*ciṭhṭhīāṇ*	*bhejdā hai*

Using the "Present Tense Chart" on page 20 you can now complete steps 5 – 6 on the worksheet. All the necessary vocabulary is at the bottom of the page. After completing the worksheet, you can use the answer sheet to check your sentences. Each lesson has an answer sheet for the worksheet on the last page of the lesson.

The Think and Speak Method

Daily practice exercises are included with each lesson so that you can immediately apply what you are learning. The accompanying practice calendar is for tracking your progress for a month, so it is recommended to spend sufficient time practicing each lesson before moving on to the next lesson. Remember, the goal of this course is not simply to learn grammar but to start speaking Punjabi by putting theory into practice.

The daily practice exercises use the 'think and speak' method. Rather than writing out the answers, you will be asked to think about the answer and then say it out loud. It can be said that to learn to read, you need to practice reading. To learn to write, you need to practice writing. But to learn to speak, you need to practice speaking.

There is no answer sheet provided for the daily practice exercises. This encourages you to go back to the lesson and its accompanying charts for confirmation. The daily exercises can be done either individually or with a partner.

We recommend a daily practice sessions of approximately 15 minutes. Research has shown that brief but frequent practice sessions are far more beneficial than long but infrequent sessions. When you feel comfortable with performing the exercises then you are ready to move on to the next lesson and build larger sentences!

LESSON ONE VOCABULARY

1. Words with masculine gender are highlighted in blue.
2. Words with feminine gender are highlighted in pink.
3. Words that are used for both the singular and plural form are marked with (s).

am/are ਹਾਂ *hāṇ*	answer(s) ਜਵਾਬ *javāb*	are ਹੋ *ho*
are ਹਨ *han*	to ask ਪੁੱਛਣਾ *puchchṇā*	English ਅੰਗਰੇਜ਼ੀ *aṇgrezī*
he/she/they/that ਉਹ *uh*	I ਮੈਂ *maiṇ*	is ਹੈ *hai*
to learn ਸਿੱਖਣਾ *sikhkhṇā*	picture ਤਸਵੀਰ *tasvīr*	Punjabi ਪੰਜਾਬੀ *paṇjābī*
question(s) ਸਵਾਲ *savāl*	to see ਦੇਖਣਾ *dekhṇā*	to speak ਬੋਲਣਾ *bolṇā*
we ਅਸੀਂ *āsīṇ*	to write ਲਿਖਣਾ *likhṇā*	you ਤੁਸੀਂ *tusīṇ*

LESSON ONE WORKSHEET

Step one: Ask **what is being done?** (Write "V" for verb above the word)

Step two: Ask **who is doing it?** (Write "S" for subject above the word)

Step three: Ask **...what?** (Write "D.O" for direct object above the word)

Step four: Write the English words in the Punjabi word order on the first line

Step five: Write the Punjabi words underneath on the second line.

Step six: Add the appropriate verb ending and auxiliary verb.

S V D.O.
1. I learn Punjabi. I Punjabi learn.

ਮੈਂ ਪੰਜਾਬੀ ਸਿੱਖਦਾ

2. We ask a question. ________________

3. I speak English. ________________

4. He writes the answer. ________________

5. You see the picture. ________________

Vocabulary: am/are ਹਾਂ | answer ਜਵਾਬ | are ਹੋ or ਹਨ | to ask ਪੁੱਛਣਾ | English ਅੰਗਰੇਜ਼ੀ
he ਉਹ | I ਮੈਂ | is ਹੈ | to learn ਸਿੱਖਣਾ | picture ਤਸਵੀਰ | Punjabi ਪੰਜਾਬੀ | question ਸਵਾਲ
to see ਦੇਖਣਾ | to speak ਬੋਲਣਾ | we ਅਸੀਂ | to write ਲਿਖਣਾ | you ਤੁਸੀਂ

PRESENT TENSE CHART

VERB ROOTS ENDING WITH CONSONANTS

SUBJECT + VERB ROOT + ENDING + AUX.VERB

Pronoun English	Pronoun Punjabi	Masculine Endings	Feminine Endings	Auxiliary Verb
I	ਮੈਂ	ਬੋਲਦਾ	ਬੋਲਦੀ	ਹਾਂ
He/She (Singular)	ਉਹ			ਹੈ
They (Plural)	ਉਹ	ਬੋਲਦੇ	ਬੋਲਦੀਆਂ	ਹਨ
We	ਅਸੀਂ	ਬੋਲਦੇ		ਹਾਂ
You	ਤੁਸੀਂ			ਹੋ

NOTE: If the subject is NOT a pronoun then determine its gender and number. The same endings for (He/She) are used for singular subjects. The same endings for (They) are used for plural subjects.

DAILY PRACTICE SHEET VOCABULARY

to ask ਪੁੱਛਣਾ *puchchṇā*	to become ਬਣਨਾ *baṇnā*	to believe/accept ਮੰਨਣਾ *maṇnṇā*
to change ਬਦਲਣਾ *badalṇā*	to come out ਨਿਕਲਣਾ *nikalṇā*	to find ਲੱਭਣਾ *labhbhṇā*
to know ਜਾਣਨਾ *jāṇnā*	to learn ਸਿੱਖਣਾ *sikhkhṇā*	to listen/hear ਸੁਣਨਾ *suṇnā*
to meet ਮਿਲਣਾ *milṇā*	to open ਖੋਲ੍ਹਣਾ *kholhṇā*	to put/keep ਰੱਖਣਾ *rakhkhṇā*
to read ਪੜ੍ਹਨਾ *paṛhnā*	to see ਦੇਖਣਾ *dekhṇā*	to sit ਬੈਠਣਾ *baiṭhṇā*
to speak/talk ਬੋਲਣਾ *bolṇā*	to tell ਦੱਸਣਾ *dassṇā*	to think ਸੋਚਣਾ *socṇā*
to understand ਸਮਝਣਾ *samajhṇā*	to walk ਤੁਰਨਾ *turnā*	to write ਲਿਖਣਾ *likhṇā*

DAILY PRACTICE SHEET

Instructions for the 'Think and Speak' method:

Do NOT write down the answers – this is the 'think' part

Say each sentence OUT LOUD – this is the 'speak' part

What if I get stuck? Look at the reference charts for help. The goal is NOT to 'memorize' the sentences but to LEARN A METHOD to construct your own sentences.

SUBJECT + DIRECT OBJECT + VERB ROOT + ENDING + AUX.VERB

Exercise One: The Basic Sentence

Say each sentence OUT LOUD.

1. He asks.

ਉਹ + ਪੁੱਛ + ending + aux.verb

= ਉਹ ਪੁੱਛਦਾ ਹੈ

2. We become.
3. They believe/accept.
4. I change.
5. She emerges/comes out.
6. You find.
7. He knows.
8. We learn.
9. They listen/hear.
10. I meet.
11. She opens.
12. You put/keep.
13. He reads.
14. We see.
15. They ask.
16. I sit.
17. She talks/speaks.
18. You tell.
19. He thinks.
20. We understand.
21. They walk.
22. I write.
23. She asks.
24. You become.
25. He believes/accepts.
26. We change.
27. They emerge/come out.
28. I find.
29. She knows.
30. You learn.
31. He listens/hears.
32. We meet.
33. They open.
34. I put/keep.
35. She reads.
36. You see.
37. He sits.
38. We talk/speak.
39. They tell.
40. I think.
41. She understands.
42. You walk.
43. He writes.

Exercise Two: Sentence Progressions

Add a DIRECT OBJECT of your choice to the sentences from exercise one and say each sentence OUT LOUD. Skip the sentences shaded in gray because they do not take a direct object easily. To get started, here is a list of direct objects in English.

TIP: For this exercise, we will use English words for our objects. Starting in lesson two, we will use Punjabi words for our objects.

answer	book(s)	cars
cat	chairs	door(s)
English	friend(s)	gifts
house(s)	letters	magazines
movie	pathway	picture(s)
price	Punjabi	question
reason(s)	shop	song(s)
stories	story	work

Exercise Three: Quick Start

Say each sentence using the SAME subject. (e.g. we, I, he, Nick, they, she, you)

1. __ ask(s)
2. __ become(s)
3. __ believe/accept(s)
4. __ change(s)
5. __ emerge(s)/come(s) out
6. __ find(s)
7. __ know(s)
8. __ learn(s)
9. __ listen/hear(s)
10. __ meet(s)
11. __ open(s)
12. __ put/keep(s)
13. __ read(s)
14. __ see(s)
15. __ sit(s)
16. __ speak/talk(s)
17. __ tell(s)
18. __ think(s)
19. __ understand(s)
20. __ walk(s)
21. __ write(s)

PRACTICE CALENDAR

Box 1: Practice 5 minutes or more of exercise one and then ✓ check box 1

Box 2: Practice 5 minutes or more of exercise two and then ✓ check box 2

Box 3: Practice 5 minutes or more of exercise three and then ✓ check box 3

	Week 1			Week 2			Week 3			Week 4		
Monday	1	2	3	1	2	3	1	2	3	1	2	3
Tuesday	1	2	3	1	2	3	1	2	3	1	2	3
Wednesday	1	2	3	1	2	3	1	2	3	1	2	3
Thursday	1	2	3	1	2	3	1	2	3	1	2	3
Friday	1	2	3	1	2	3	1	2	3	1	2	3
Saturday	1	2	3	1	2	3	1	2	3	1	2	3
Sunday	1	2	3	1	2	3	1	2	3	1	2	3

WORKSHEET ANSWERS

Step one: Ask **what is being done?** (Write "V" for verb above the word)

Step two: Ask **who is doing it?** (Write "S" for subject above the word)

Step three: Ask **...what?** (Write "D.O" for direct object above the word)

Step four: Write the English words in the Punjabi word order on the first line

Step five: Write the Punjabi words underneath on the second line.

Step six: Add the appropriate verb ending and auxiliary verb.

S V D.O.
1. I learn Punjabi.

I Punjabi learn

ਮੈਂ ਪੰਜਾਬੀ ਸਿੱਖਦਾ ਹਾਂ (masculine subject)
ਮੈਂ ਪੰਜਾਬੀ ਸਿੱਖਦੀ ਹਾਂ (feminine subject)

S V D.O.
2. We ask ~~a~~ question.

We questions ask

ਅਸੀਂ ਸਵਾਲ ਪੁੱਛਦੇ ਹਾਂ

S V D.O.
3. I speak English.

I English speak

ਮੈਂ ਅੰਗਰੇਜ਼ੀ ਬੋਲਦਾ ਹਾਂ (masculine subject)
ਮੈਂ ਅੰਗਰੇਜ਼ੀ ਬੋਲਦੀ ਹਾਂ (feminine subject)

S V D.O.
4. He writes ~~the~~ answer.

He answer writes

ਉਹ ਜਵਾਬ ਲਿਖਦਾ ਹੈ

S V D.O.
5. You see ~~the~~ picture.

You picture see

ਤੁਸੀਂ ਤਸਵੀਰ ਦੇਖਦੇ ਹੋ

Vocabulary: am/are ਹਾਂ | answer ਜਵਾਬ | are ਹੋ or ਹਨ | to ask ਪੁੱਛਣਾ | English ਅੰਗਰੇਜ਼ੀ
he ਉਹ | I ਮੈਂ | is ਹੈ | to learn ਸਿੱਖਣਾ | picture ਤਸਵੀਰ | Punjabi ਪੰਜਾਬੀ | question ਸਵਾਲ
to see ਦੇਖਣਾ | to speak ਬੋਲਣਾ | we ਅਸੀਂ | to write ਲਿਖਣਾ | you ਤੁਸੀਂ

LESSON TWO

INDIRECT OBJECTS

Position Words

Often sentences include more than one object. To accomplish this, we need to use some small but very important words called position words.

Position words include such words as: in, from, on, for, about, with, than & to.
In English these position words are called prepositions because they come before the noun. In Punjabi they are called postpositions because they come after the noun.

For example, in English we say "with Nick" but in Punjabi we say "Nick with."

Indirect Objects

Whenever we add a position word to an object it becomes a special type of object called an indirect object. Any object without a position word, which we learned about in lesson one, is called a direct object. For example, 'book' is a direct object, whereas 'in the book' is an indirect object.

Consider this example sentence: "Nick sends letters to Sonia"

SUBJECT	INDIRECT OBJECT	DIRECT OBJECT	VERB + AUX.VERB
Nick	Sonia to	letters	sends is
ਨਿਕ	ਸੋਨੀਆ ਨੂੰ	ਚਿੱਠੀਆਂ	ਭੇਜਦਾ ਹੈ
Nik	*Sonīā nūṇ*	*ciṭhṭhīāṇ*	*bhejdā hai*

As shown above, the indirect object always comes BEFORE the direct object.

In lesson one, we learned that the subject, direct object and verb are the main parts of a sentence. The indirect object is the fourth main part of a sentence. You can put one or more words into each box. To determine which box to put a word into, ask the following questions:

1. Identify the **VERB** by asking: **What is being done?**
2. Identify the **SUBJECT** by asking: **Who is doing it?**
3. Identify the **DIRECT OBJECT** by asking: **...what?**
4. Identify the **INDIRECT OBJECT** by asking: **TO what? TO whom?**
   FOR what? FOR whom?
   WITH what? WITH whom?

NOTE: The **INDIRECT OBJECT** can be identified using ANY position word.

In English, sometimes the position word is dropped. For example, the sentence "Nick sends Sonia letters" is the same as "Nick sends letters to Sonia." In both sentences 'Sonia' is the indirect object. However, in the first sentence the position word 'to' is dropped.

In Punjabi, the key is to remember that whenever you are using people as objects, you must ALWAYS use a position word. When in doubt, use the position word ("to" ਨੂੰ *nūṇ*).

So it is helpful to REWORD the English sentence, as shown above, to include the position word before translating it.

If the indirect object still seems unclear, try PERSONALIZING the questions from the previous page. For example: What does Nick send? Does Nick send 'letters' or 'Sonia'? Nick sends letters. (This is the direct object) To whom does Nick send letters? To Sonia (This is the indirect object)

Putting Theory into Practice

At this point, find page 30 entitled "Lesson Two Worksheet." This worksheet has five sentences for you to translate. Go ahead and translate sentences 1-2.

Oblique Nouns

To master the use of position words we need to consider one more thing. Any noun joined with a postposition is in the indirect or 'oblique' form. In English, pronouns change their spelling in the oblique form. For example, we cannot say "The letter is for we." Instead, we say "The letter is for us."

"I" changes to "me"
"he" changes to "him"
"she" changes to "her"
"we" changes to "us"
"they" changes to "them"

In Punjabi, pronouns in the oblique form also undergo changes. The reference chart "How Postpositions Change Pronouns" on page 31 shows how pronouns change when followed by postpositions.

In addition to pronouns, most MASCULINE NOUNS change in the oblique form. The reference chart "How Postpositions Change Masculine Nouns" on page 32 shows how masculine nouns change when followed by postpositions.

Using these two reference charts, go ahead and complete sentences 3-5 on the worksheet.

When you feel comfortable with performing the daily exercises then you are ready to move on to the next lesson and build larger sentences!

LESSON TWO VOCABULARY

1. Words with masculine gender are highlighted in blue.
2. Words with feminine gender are highlighted in pink.
3. Words that are used for both the singular and plural form are marked with (s).

about ਬਾਰੇ *bāre*	book ਕਿਤਾਬ *kitāb*	door ਦਰਵਾਜ਼ਾ *darvāzā*
for ਲਈ *laī*	from ਤੋਂ *toṇ*	in ਵਿੱਚ *vicc*
my ਮੇਰਾ *merā*	of ਦਾ *dā*	on ਉੱਤੇ *utte*
our ਸਾਡਾ *sāḍhā*	songs(s) ਗੀਤ *gīt*	story ਕਹਾਣੀ *kahāṇī*
to ਨੂੰ *nūṇ*	to me ਮੈਨੂੰ *mainūṇ*	to us ਸਾਨੂੰ *sānūṇ*
to you ਤੁਹਾਨੂੰ *tuhānūṇ*	with ਨਾਲ *nāl*	your ਤੁਹਾਡਾ *tuhāḍhā*

LESSON TWO WORKSHEET

Step one: Ask **what is being done?** (Write "V" for verb above the word)
Step two: Ask **who is doing it?** (Write "S" for subject above the word)
Step three: Ask **...what?** (Write "d.O" for direct object above the word)
Step four: Ask **TO what? TO whom?** (Write "i.O" for indirect object above the word)
Step four: Write the English words in the Punjabi word order on the first line
Step five: Write the Punjabi words underneath on the second line.
Step six: Add the appropriate verb ending and auxiliary verb.

1. He opens the door for us. ______________________

____

2. I see a picture in the book. ______________________

____

3. We learn songs from a friend. (masculine noun) ______________________

____

4. She reads a story for them. (pronoun) ______________________

____

5. They keep the letters for me. (pronoun) ______________________

____

Vocabulary: am ਹਾਂ | are ਹਨ | book ਕਿਤਾਬ (feminine) | door ਦਰਵਾਜ਼ਾ | for ਲਈ
friend(s) ਦੋਸਤ (masc.) | from ਤੋਂ | he/she ਉਹ | I ਮੈਂ | in ਵਿੱਚ | is ਹੈ | to keep ਰੱਖਣਾ
to learn ਸਿੱਖਣਾ | letters ਚਿੱਠੀਆਂ | to open ਖੋਲ੍ਹਣਾ | picture ਤਸਵੀਰ | to read ਪੜ੍ਹਨਾ
to see ਦੇਖਣਾ | song(s) ਗੀਤ | story ਕਹਾਣੀ | they ਉਹ | we ਅਸੀਂ

HOW POSTPOSITIONS CHANGE PRONOUNS

Pronoun in English	In Punjabi	Pronoun followed by the postposition ਨੂੰ	Pronoun followed by any other postposition (ie.ਤੋਂ)
I	ਮੈਂ	ਮੈਨੂੰ	ਮੇਰੇ ਤੋਂ
We	ਅਸੀਂ	ਸਾਨੂੰ	ਸਾਡੇ ਤੋਂ
You	ਤੁਸੀਂ	ਤੁਹਾਨੂੰ	ਤੁਹਾਡੇ ਤੋਂ
This (singular, near)	ਇਹ	ਇਹ ਨੂੰ or ਇਸ ਨੂੰ	ਇਸ ਤੋਂ
He/She/That (singular, far)	ਉਹ	ਉਹ ਨੂੰ or ਉਸ ਨੂੰ	ਉਸ ਤੋਂ
These (plural, near)	ਇਹ	ਇਹਨਾਂ ਨੂੰ	ਇਹਨਾਂ ਤੋਂ
They/Those (plural, far)	ਉਹ	ਉਹਨਾਂ ਨੂੰ	ਉਹਨਾਂ ਤੋਂ

HOW POSTPOSITIONS CHANGE MASCULINE NOUNS

Masculine Nouns - With Vowel Endings			
Singular (ends with ਾ)	son ਬੇਟਾ	to son ਬੇਟੇ ਨੂੰ	**ਾ becomes ੇ** (The meaning "to son" does not change)
Plural (ends with ੇ)	sons ਬੇਟੇ	to sons ਬੇਟਿਆਂ ਨੂੰ	**ੇ becomes ਿਆਂ** (The meaning "to sons" does not change)

Masculine Nouns - No Vowel Endings			
Singular	friend ਦੋਸਤ	to friend ਦੋਸਤ ਨੂੰ	**No change** (The meaning "to friend" does not change)
Plural	friends ਦੋਸਤ	to friends ਦੋਸਤਾਂ ਨੂੰ	**Add ਾਂ** (The meaning "to friends" does not change)

DAILY PRACTICE SHEET VOCABULARY

1. Words with masculine gender are highlighted in blue
2. Words with feminine gender are highlighted in pink.
3. Words that are used for both the singular and plural form are marked with (s).

books ਕਿਤਾਬਾਂ *kitābāṇ*	cars ਗੱਡੀਆਂ *gaḍḍīāṇ*	cat ਬਿੱਲੀ *billī*
chairs ਕੁਰਸੀਆਂ *kursiāṇ*	doors ਦਰਵਾਜੇ *darvāje*	friend(s) ਦੋਸਤ *dost*
gifts ਤੋਹਫ਼ੇ *tohfe*	house(s) ਘਰ *ghar*	letters ਚਿੱਠੀਆਂ *ciṭhṭhīāṇ*
magazines ਰਸਾਲੇ *rasāle*	movie/film ਫਿਲਮ *film*	pathway(s) ਰਾਹ *rāh*
pictures ਤਸਵੀਰਾਂ *tasvīrāṇ*	price ਕੀਮਤ *kīmat*	reason(s) ਕਾਰਨ *kāran*
shop ਦੁਕਾਨ *dukān*	stories ਕਹਾਣੀਆਂ *kahāṇīāṇ*	work ਕੰਮ *kaṇm*

DAILY PRACTICE SHEET

Instructions for the 'Think and Speak' method:

Do NOT write down the answers – this is the 'think' part

Say each sentence OUT LOUD – this is the 'speak' part

What if I get stuck? Look at the reference charts for help. The goal is NOT to 'memorize' the sentences but to LEARN A METHOD to construct your own sentences.

SUBJECT + DIRECT OBJECT + VERB ROOT + ENDING + AUX.VERB

Exercise One: Direct Objects

Say each sentence OUT LOUD using the Punjabi vocabulary.

1. He asks a question.
= ਉਹ ਸਵਾਲ ਪੁੱਛਦਾ ਹੈ
2. We become friends.
3. They believe/accept the answer.
4. I change the price.
5. She finds a pathway.
6. You know the reason.
7. He learns English.
8. We hear a song.
9. They open the door.
10. I keep the chairs.
11. She reads the magazines.
12. You see a house.
13. He speaks Punjabi.
14. We tell the story.
15. They understand the movie.
16. I write books.
17. She asks a question.
18. You change the pictures.
19. He finds a car.
20. We know the price.
21. They learn the work.
22. I open the gifts.
23. She keeps the cat.
24. You read the letters.
25. He sees the shop.
26. We speak English.
27. They tell the reason.
28. I understand Punjabi.
29. You write the answer.

Exercise Two: Indirect Objects

Say each sentence OUT LOUD. Remember to use the charts on pages 31 - 32.

1. He asks about us.

= ਉਹ ਸਾਡੇ ਬਾਰੇ ਪੁੱਛਦਾ ਹੈ

Note: ਅਸੀਂ + ਬਾਰੇ = ਸਾਡੇ ਬਾਰ

3. We emerge from the shop.
3. They sit on chairs.
4. I meet with a friend.
5. She listens to me.
6. You think about the question.
7. He walks on the pathway.
8. We emerge from the house.
9. They tell about the movie.
10. I write in the book.
11. She learns with them.
12. You change for her.
13. He reads to me.
14. We meet in the shop.

Exercise Three: Sentence Progressions

Say the sentences from EXERCISE ONE with an INDIRECT OBJECT of your choice.

PRONOUN/OBJECT + POSITION WORD = INDIRECT OBJECT

Pronouns	Objects		
him	answer	book(s)	cars
us	cat	chairs	door(s)
them	English	friend(s)	gifts
you	house(s)	letters	magazines
me	movie	pathway	picture(s)
she	price	Punjabi	question
	reason(s)	shop	song(s)
	stories	story	work

\+

Position Words
from
in
on
with
for
about
to

PRACTICE CALENDAR

Box 1: Practice 5 minutes or more of exercise one and then ✓ check box 1

Box 2: Practice 5 minutes or more of exercise two and then ✓ check box 2

Box 3: Practice 5 minutes or more of exercise three and then ✓ check box 3

	Week 1			Week 2			Week 3			Week 4		
Monday	1	2	3	1	2	3	1	2	3	1	2	3
Tuesday	1	2	3	1	2	3	1	2	3	1	2	3
Wednesday	1	2	3	1	2	3	1	2	3	1	2	3
Thursday	1	2	3	1	2	3	1	2	3	1	2	3
Friday	1	2	3	1	2	3	1	2	3	1	2	3
Saturday	1	2	3	1	2	3	1	2	3	1	2	3
Sunday	1	2	3	1	2	3	1	2	3	1	2	3

WORKSHEET ANSWERS

Step one: Ask **what is being done?** (Write "V" for verb above the word)

Step two: Ask **who is doing it?** (Write "S" for subject above the word)

Step three: Ask **...what?** (Write "d.O" for direct object above the word)

Step four: Ask **TO what? TO whom?** (Write "i.O" for indirect object above the word)

Step four: Write the English words in the Punjabi word order on the first line

Step five: Write the Punjabi words underneath on the second line.

Step six: Add the appropriate verb ending and auxiliary verb.

S V D.O. I.O.

1. He opens the door for us. He us for door opens

ਉਹ ਸਾਡੇ ਲਈ ਦਰਵਾਜ਼ਾ ਖੋਲ੍ਹਦਾ ਹੈ

S V D.O. I.O.

2. I see a picture in the book. I book in picture see

ਮੈਂ ਕਿਤਾਬ ਵਿੱਚ ਤਸਵੀਰ ਦੇਖਦਾ ਹਾਂ (masculine subject)

ਮੈਂ ਕਿਤਾਬ ਵਿੱਚ ਤਸਵੀਰ ਦੇਖਦੀ ਹਾਂ (feminine subject)

S V D.O. I.O.

3. We learn songs from a friend. We friend from songs learn

ਅਸੀਂ ਦੋਸਤਾਂ ਤੋਂ ਗੀਤ ਸਿੱਖਦੇ ਹਾਂ

S V D.O. I.O.

4. She reads a story for them. She them for story reads

ਉਹ ਉਹਨਾਂ ਲਈ ਕਹਾਣੀ ਪੜ੍ਹਦੀ ਹੈ

S V D.O. I.O.

5. They keep the letters for me. They me for letters keep

ਉਹ ਮੇਰੇ ਲਈ ਚਿੱਠੀਆਂ ਰੱਖਦੇ ਹਨ

Vocabulary: am ਹਾਂ | are ਹਨ | book ਕਿਤਾਬ (feminine) | door ਦਰਵਾਜ਼ਾ | for ਲਈ friend(s) ਦੋਸਤ (masc.) | from ਤੋਂ | he/she ਉਹ | I ਮੈਂ | in ਵਿੱਚ | is ਹੈ | to keep ਰੱਖਣਾ to learn ਸਿੱਖਣਾ | letters ਚਿੱਠੀਆਂ | to open ਖੋਲ੍ਹਣਾ | picture ਤਸਵੀਰ | to read ਪੜ੍ਹਨਾ to see ਦੇਖਣਾ | song(s) ਗੀਤ | story ਕਹਾਣੀ | they ਉਹ | we ਅਸੀਂ

LESSON THREE

CONNECTING SENTENCES

Connecting Words

A key to success in speaking Punjabi depends on understanding one important fact: In Punjabi, it is COMMON, sometimes even necessary, to use SHORT SENTENCES. This principle cannot be overemphasized.

Breaking a long sentence into smaller sentences ALWAYS makes speaking easier, so here is a helpful guideline:

If you CAN break up a sentence into smaller sentences – then BREAK IT UP!

Short sentences can then be joined together with these common connecting words: because, and, but, that, then, if & when.

In English, we often drop the connecting words. For example, we might say "I know she reads Punjabi." In this sentence, there are two actions 'know' and 'read' being done by two different people 'I know' and 'she reads.' In Punjabi this sentence MUST be broken into two parts using a connecting word: "I know <u>that</u> she reads Punjabi."

Let's look at some more example sentences. In the following two examples, the connecting word goes between the two sentences.

1. I read Punjabi <u>and</u> they read English.
2. I can speak Punjabi <u>but</u> I cannot speak Hindi.

There are also some connecting words that are used in pairs.

1. <u>If</u> I learn Punjabi <u>then</u> I can understand you.
2. <u>When</u> I learn Punjabi <u>then</u> you are happy.

Verb Roots Ending with Vowels & Irregular Verbs

There are a handful of verbs that follow an irregular construction in the present tense. These can be found in the reference chart "Irregular Verbs - Present Tense" on page 46.

This lesson includes new vocabulary on page 47 for the daily practice exercises. This new vocabulary sheet gives verb roots that end in vowels. See reference charts "Verb Roots Ending in Kanna" on page 44 and "Verb Roots Ending in Other Vowels" on page 45 when practicing.

At this point, find page 43 entitled "Lesson Three Worksheet." Go ahead and complete sentence one.

You will notice in the example sentences on page 38 that we introduced three new elements (1)the word 'not' (2) the verb 'can' and (3) a descriptive sentence. Let's learn how to do this in Punjabi.

Descriptive Sentences

Descriptive Sentences are the easiest sentences because they only include one verb. There is no action taking place, rather, we are describing something. For example: "The letter is interesting."

SUBJECT	COMPLEMENT	VERB
letter	interesting	is
ਚਿੱਠੀ	ਦਿਲਚਸਪ	ਹੈ
ciṭhṭhī	*dilcasp*	*hai*

Go ahead and complete sentence 2 on the worksheet.

Negative Sentences

In English, negative sentences use an auxiliary verb in front of the word 'not' to show whether the action is past, present or future tense. For example:

> "Nick did not send letters"
>
> "Nick does not send letters"
>
> "Nick will not send letters"

In Punjabi, this is unnecessary as there is already an auxiliary verb at the end of the sentence. So to form a negative sentence simply insert the word ਨਹੀਂ *nahīṇ* (not) and ignore the extra auxiliary verb. For example: "Nick ~~does~~ not send letters."

SUBJECT	DIRECT OBJECT	VERB + AUX.VERB
Nick	letters	not send is
ਨਿਕ	ਚਿੱਠੀਆਂ	ਨਹੀਂ ਭੇਜਦਾ ਹੈ
Nik	*ciṭhṭhīāṇ*	*nahīṇ bhejdā hai*

As shown in the verb box, the word ਨਹੀਂ *nahīṇ* (not) goes before the MAIN verb in the sentence. Go ahead and complete sentence 3 on the worksheet.

Ability

Ability to carry out an action is expressed through the verb ਸਕਣਾ *sakṇā* (to be able/ can). Similar to English, ਸਕਣਾ *sakṇā* (can) is always used with the ROOT of another verb. In English, the word can (ਸਕਣਾ *sakṇā*) comes before the root. In Punjabi, the word ਸਕਣਾ *sakṇā* (can) comes after the root. It should not be attached to the root.

In every other way, ਸਕਣਾ *sakṇā* behaves like all the other verbs. For example, it changes according to the number and gender of the subject.

For example: "Nick **can** send letters." (lit. "Nick **is able** to send letters.")

SUBJECT	DIRECTOBJECT	VERB + AUX.VERB
Nick	letters	send can is
ਨਿਕ	ਚਿੱਠੀਆਂ	ਭੇਜ ਸਕਦਾ ਹੈ
Nik	*ciṭhṭhīāṇ*	*bhej sakdā hai*

To make a negative sentence, simply insert the word ਨਹੀ (not) before the verb.

For example: "Nick cannot send letters."

SUBJECT	DIRECTOBJECT	VERB + AUX.VERB
Nick	letters	not send can is
ਨਿਕ	ਚਿੱਠੀਆਂ	ਨਹੀਂ ਭੇਜ ਸਕਦਾ ਹੈ
Nik	*ciṭhṭhīāṇ*	*nahīṇ bhej sakdā hai*

Go ahead and complete sentences 4 & 5 on the worksheet.

The daily practice sheet in this lesson contains six exercises. We will divide the fifteen minutes of practice between these six exercises. It is important to spend at least a few minutes on each exercise.

When you feel comfortable with performing the daily exercises then you are ready to move on to the next lesson and build larger sentences!

LESSON THREE VOCABULARY

1. Words with masculine gender are highlighted in blue.
2. Words with feminine gender are highlighted in pink.
3. Words that are used for both the singular and plural form are marked with (s).

and ਅਤੇ or ਤੇ *āte or te*	beautiful ਸੁੰਦਰ *suṇdar*	because ਕਿਉਂਕਿ *kiuṇki*
but ਪਰ *par*	can / to be able ਸਕਣਾ *sakṇā*	to eat ਖਾਣਾ *khāṇā*
far ਦੂਰ *dūr*	food/meal(s) ਭੋਜਨ *bhojan*	happy ਖੁਸ਼ *kush*
to give ਦੇਣਾ *deṇā*	if ਜੇ *je*	interesting ਦਿਲਚਸਪ *dilcasp*
not ਨਹੀਂ *nahīṇ*	quiet ਚੁੱਪ *cupp*	red ਲਾਲ *lāl*
that ਕਿ *ki*	then ਤਾਂ *tāṇ*	when ਜਦੋਂ *jadoṇ*

LESSON THREE WORKSHEET

Step one: Ask **what is being done?** (Write "V" for verb above the word)

Step two: Ask **who is doing it?** (Write "S" for subject above the word)

Step three: Ask **...what?** (Write "d.O" for direct object above the word)

Step four: Ask **TO what? TO whom?** (Write "i.O" for indirect object above the word)

Step four: Write the English words in the Punjabi word order on the first line

Step five: Write the Punjabi words underneath on the second line.

Step six: Add the appropriate verb ending and auxiliary verb.

1. We eat because she gives food to us. ______________________

____

2. I know that the movie is interesting. ______________________

____

3. If you do not listen then you do not learn. ______________________

____

4. We learn Punjabi and we can understand him. ______________________

____

5. He can speak Punjabi but he cannot read Punjabi. ______________________

____

Vocabulary: and ਅਤੇ | are ਹੋ | am ਹਾਂ | because ਕਿਉਂਕਿ | but ਪਰ | can ਸਕਣਾ | eat ਖਾਣਾ food ਭੋਜਨ | gives ਦੇਣਾ | he/she ਉਹ | I ਮੈਂ | if ਜੇ | interesting ਦਲਿਚਸਪ | is ਹ | to know ਜਾਣਨਾ learn ਸਿੱਖਣਾ | listen ਸੁਣਨਾ | movie ਫਿਲਮ | not ਨਹੀਂ | Punjabi ਪੰਜਾਬੀ | read ਪੜ੍ਹਨਾ | speak ਬੋਲਣਾ that ਕਿ | then ਤਾਂ | to ਨੂੰ | understand ਸਮਝਣਾ | we ਅਸੀਂ | you ਤੁਸੀਂ

PRESENT TENSE CHART
VERB ROOTS ENDING WITH KANNA

SUBJECT + VERB ROOT + ENDING + AUX.VERB

<table>
<tr><th>Pronoun English</th><th>Pronoun Punjabi</th><th>Masculine Endings</th><th>Feminine Endings</th><th>Auxilliary Verb</th></tr>
<tr><td>I</td><td>ਮੈਂ</td><td rowspan="2">ਆਉਂਦਾ</td><td rowspan="2">ਆਉਂਦੀ</td><td>ਹਾਂ</td></tr>
<tr><td>He/She (Singular)</td><td>ਉਹ</td><td>ਹੈ</td></tr>
<tr><td>They (Plural)</td><td>ਉਹ</td><td>ਆਉਂਦੇ</td><td>ਆਉਂਦੀਆਂ</td><td>ਹਨ</td></tr>
<tr><td>We</td><td>ਅਸੀਂ</td><td colspan="2" rowspan="2">ਆਉਂਦੇ</td><td>ਹਾਂ</td></tr>
<tr><td>You</td><td>ਤੁਸੀਂ</td><td>ਹੋ</td></tr>
</table>

NOTE: If the subject is NOT a pronoun then determine its gender and number. The same endings for (He/She) are used for singular subjects. The same endings for (They) are used for plural subjects.

PRESENT TENSE CHART

VERB ROOTS ENDING WITH OTHER VOWELS

SUBJECT + VERB ROOT + ENDING + AUX.VERB

<table>
<tr><th>Pronoun English</th><th>Pronoun Punjabi</th><th>Masculine Endings</th><th>Feminine Endings</th><th>Auxiliary Verb</th></tr>
<tr><td>I</td><td>ਮੈਂ</td><td rowspan="2">ਲੈਂਦਾ</td><td rowspan="2">ਲੈਂਦੀ</td><td>ਹਾਂ</td></tr>
<tr><td>He/She (Singular)</td><td>ਉਹ</td><td>ਹੈ</td></tr>
</table>

<table>
<tr><td>They (Plural)</td><td>ਉਹ</td><td>ਲੈਂਦੇ</td><td>ਲੈਂਦੀਆਂ</td><td>ਹਨ</td></tr>
</table>

<table>
<tr><td>We</td><td>ਅਸੀਂ</td><td rowspan="2" colspan="2">ਲੈਂਦੇ</td><td>ਹਾਂ</td></tr>
<tr><td>You</td><td>ਤੁਸੀਂ</td><td>ਹੋ</td></tr>
</table>

NOTE: If the subject is NOT a pronoun then determine its gender and number. The same endings for (He/She) are used for singular subjects. The same endings for (They) are used for plural subjects.

IRREGULAR VERBS - PRESENT TENSE

If the verb root ends in a ਹ insert a tippee ੰ before the ending		
to want/wish ਚਾਹੁਣਾ *cāhuṇā* ਚਾਹੁੰਦਾ m/s	to reside/remain ਰਹਿਣਾ *rahiṇā* ਰਹਿੰਦਾ m/s	to say ਕਹਿਣਾ *kahiṇā* ਕਹਿੰਦਾ m/s
to touch ਛੋਹਣਾ *chohṇā* ਛੋਹੰਦਾ m/s	to be/happen ਹੋਣਾ *hoṇā* ਹੁੰਦਾ m/s	

These two verbs ending with kanna are exceptions to the rule. Insert only a bindee ਂ before the ending		Replace vowel and insert a tippee ੰ before the ending
to go ਜਾਣਾ *jāṇā* ਜਾਂਦਾ m/s	to eat ਖਾਣਾ *khāṇā* ਖਾਂਦਾ m/s	to give ਦੇਣਾ *deṇā* ਦਿੰਦਾ m/s

DAILY PRACTICE SHEET VOCABULARY

VERB ROOTS ENDING WITH KANNA

to achieve/put on ਪਾਉਣਾ *pāuṇā*	to bring ਲਿਆਉਣਾ *liāuṇā*	to call/summon ਬੁਲਾਉਣਾ *bulāuṇā*
to come ਆਉਣਾ *āuṇā*	to drive ਚਲਾਉਣਾ *calāuṇā*	to explain ਸਮਝਾਉਣਾ *samjhāuṇā*
to lose ਗੁਆਉਣਾ *guāuṇā*	to make ਬਣਾਉਣਾ *banāuṇā*	to save/rescue ਬਚਾਉਣਾ *bacāuṇā*
to show ਦਿਖਾਉਣਾ *dikhāuṇā*	to sing ਗਾਉਣਾ *gāuṇā*	to teach ਸਿਖਾਉਣਾ *sikhāuṇā*

VERB ROOTS ENDING WITH OTHER VOWELS

to take/receive ਲੈਣਾ *laiṇā*	to drink ਪੀਣਾ *pīṇā*	to sleep ਸੌਣਾ *sauṇā*

DAILY PRACTICE SHEET

Instructions for the 'Think and Speak' method:

Do NOT write down the answers – this is the 'think' part

Say each sentence OUT LOUD – this is the 'speak' part

SUBJECT + I.OBJECT + D.OBJECT + VERB ROOT + ENDING + AUX.VERB

Exercise One: Verb Roots Ending in Kanna

1. Say each sentence OUT LOUD.

1. He puts on/achieves.

ਉਹ + ਪਾ + ending + aux.verb

= ਉਹ ਪਾਉਂਦਾ ਹੈ

2. We bring.
3. They call.
4. I come.
5. She drives.
6. You explain.
7. He loses.
8. We make.
9. They save/rescue.
10. I show.
11. She sings.
12. You teach.
13. He puts on/achieves.

Exercise Two: Irregular Verbs

1. Say each sentence OUT LOUD.

1. He wants.

= ਉਹ ਚਾਹੁੰਦਾ ਹੈ

2. We be/happen.
3. She resides/remains.
4. I say.
5. They touch.
6. You go.
7. He eats.
8. We give.
9. They want.
11. I go.
11. She gives.

Exercise Three: Verb Roots Ending in Other Vowels

1. Say each sentence OUT LOUD.

1. He takes/receives.

ਉਹ + ਲੈ + ending + aux.verb

= ਉਹ ਲੈਂਦਾ ਹੈ

2. We drink.
3. They sleep.
4. I take/receive.
5. She drinks.
6. He sleeps.
7. You take/receive.

Exercise Four: Ability & Negative Sentences

1. Say each sentence OUT LOUD.
2. Add the negative and repeat the sentence again.
3. Add an indirect OR a direct object and repeat the sentence again.

1. He can ask.

ਉਹ + ਪੁੱਛ + ਸਕ + ending + aux.

= ਉਹ ਪੁੱਛ ਸਕਦਾ ਹੈ

= ਉਹ ਨਹੀਂ ਪੁੱਛ ਸਕਦਾ ਹੈ

2. We can become.
3. They can believe/accept.
4. I can change.
5. She can emerge/come out.
6. You can find.
7. He can know.
8. We can learn.
9. I can listen/hear.
10. They can meet.
11. She can open.
12. You can put/keep.
13. He can read.
14. We can see.
15. I can sit.
16. She can talk/speak.
17. You can tell.
18. He can think.
19. We can understand.
20. They can walk.
21. You can write.

Exercise Five: Descriptive Sentences

1. Say each sentence OUT LOUD.

1. They are happy*

= ਉਹ ਖੁਸ਼ ਹਨ

2. He is not quiet.

= ਉਹ ਚੁੱਪ ਨਹੀਂ ਹੈ

3. The book is interesting.
4. The cars are far.
5. The house is not red.
6. The letter is beautiful.
7. The store is not far.
8. You are quiet.
9. The chair is red.
10. I am happy.

*Note: We can also say ਉਹ ਖੁਸ਼ ਹੁੰਦੇ ਹਨ (Lit. They be happy.)

Exercise Six: Connecting Words

Use a connecting word (and, because, but, that, then, if, when) to join together any two sentences from the practice sheet exercises (or two sentences of your own). Skip the sentences shaded in gray until lesson four.

PRACTICE CALENDAR

Box 1: Practice 5 minutes or more of exercises **1, 2 & 3** and then ✓ check box 1

Box 2: Practice 5 minutes or more of exercise **four** and then ✓ check box 2

Box 3: Practice 5 minutes or more of exercises **five & six** and then ✓ check box 3

	Week 1			Week 2			Week 3			Week 4		
Monday	1	2	3	1	2	3	1	2	3	1	2	3
Tuesday	1	2	3	1	2	3	1	2	3	1	2	3
Wednesday	1	2	3	1	2	3	1	2	3	1	2	3
Thursday	1	2	3	1	2	3	1	2	3	1	2	3
Friday	1	2	3	1	2	3	1	2	3	1	2	3
Saturday	1	2	3	1	2	3	1	2	3	1	2	3
Sunday	1	2	3	1	2	3	1	2	3	1	2	3

WORKSHEET ANSWERS

Step one: Ask **what is being done?** (Write "V" for verb above the word)
Step two: Ask **who is doing it?** (Write "S" for subject above the word)
Step three: Ask **...what?** (Write "d.O" for direct object above the word)
Step four: Ask **TO what? TO whom?** (Write "i.O" for indirect object above the word)
Step four: Write the English words in the Punjabi word order on the first line
Step five: Write the Punjabi words underneath on the second line.
Step six: Add the appropriate verb ending and auxiliary verb.

1. We eat because she gives food to us.

We eat **because** she us to food gives

ਅਸੀਂ ਖਾਂਦੇ ਹਾਂ ਕਿਉਂਕਿ ਉਹ ਸਾਨੂੰ ਭੋਜਨ ਦਿੰਦੀ ਹੈ

2. I know that ~~the~~ movie is interesting.

I know **that** movie interesting is

ਮੈ ਜਾਣਦਾ ਹਾਂ ਕਿ ਫਿਲਮ ਦਿਲਚਸਪ ਹੈ (masculine subject)
ਮੈ ਜਾਣਦੀ ਹਾਂ ਕਿ ਫਿਲਮ ਦਿਲਚਸਪ ਹੈ (feminine subject)

3. If you ~~do~~ not listen then you ~~do~~ not learn.

If you not listen **then** you not learn

ਜੇ ਤੁਸੀਂ ਨਹੀਂ ਸੁਣਦੇ ਹੋ ਤਾਂ ਤੁਸੀਂ ਨਹੀਂ ਸਿੱਖਦੇ ਹੋ

4. We learn Punjabi and we can understand him.

We Punjabi learn **and** we him understand can

ਅਸੀਂ ਪੰਜਾਬੀ ਸਿੱਖਦੇ ਹਾਂ ਅਤੇ ਅਸੀਂ ਉਸ ਨੂੰ ਸਮਝ ਸਕਦੇ ਹਾਂ

5. He can speak Punjabi but he cannot read Punjabi.

He Punjabi speak can **but** he Punjabi not read can

ਉਹ ਪੰਜਾਬੀ ਬੋਲ ਸਕਦਾ ਹੈ ਪਰ ਉਹ ਪੰਜਾਬੀ ਨਹੀਂ ਪੜ੍ਹ ਸਕਦਾ ਹੈ

Vocabulary: and ਅਤੇ | are ਹੋ | am ਹਾਂ | because ਕਿਉਂਕਿ | but ਪਰ | can ਸਕਣਾ | eat ਖਾਣਾ | food ਭੋਜਨ | gives ਦੇਣਾ | he/she ਉਹ | I ਮੈਂ | if ਜੇ | interesting ਦਲਿਚਸਪ | is ਹ | to know ਜਾਣਨਾ | learn ਸਿੱਖਣਾ | listen ਸੁਣਨਾ | movie ਫਿਲਮ | not ਨਹੀਂ | Punjabi ਪੰਜਾਬੀ | read ਪੜ੍ਹਨਾ | speak ਬੋਲਣਾ | that ਕਿ | then ਤਾਂ | to ਨੂੰ | understand ਸਮਝਣਾ | we ਅਸੀਂ | you ਤੁਸੀਂ

VERBALS

A Special Verb Form

There is a special verb form called a verbal which uses the ਣਾ *ṇā* or ਨਾ *nā* ending as shown:

ਲਿਖਣਾ *likhṇā* = to write / writing

When verbs are in this form then they can be used as the subject or object of a sentence.

Note: In English, the verbal is formed by adding 'to' or 'ing' to the root of the verb. The word 'to' has many different uses in English. We already learned that 'to' can be used as a position word. Now we see a second use for the word 'to' which is to indicate a verbal.

Verbals as Subjects

Verbals are commonly used in the subject box in descriptive sentences. Descriptive sentences use the verb 'is' as the main verb. For example: "Writing is easy."

SUBJECT	COMPLEMENT	VERB
Writing	easy	is
ਲਿਖਣਾ	ਸੌਖਾ	ਹੈ
likhṇā	*saukhā*	*hai*

Since verbals do not have gender on their own, they use the default gender which is masculine singular.

Please find page 58 entitled "Lesson Four Worksheet" and complete sentence one.

Verbals as Direct Objects

Verbals are often used in the direct object box with sentences that use the verb 'want.' For example: "Nick wants to write to Sonia" Nick wants what? 'to write' (This is the direct object) Nick wants to write to whom? 'to Sonia' (This is the indirect object)

SUBJECT	INDIRECT OBJECT	DIRECT OBJECT	VERB + AUX.VERB
Nick	Sonia to	to write	wants is
ਨਿਕ	ਸੋਨੀਆ ਨੂੰ	ਲਿਖਣਾ	ਚਾਹੁੰਦਾ ਹੈ
Nik	Sonīā nūṇ	likhṇā	cāhuṇdā hai

Remember: In English, when the word 'to' is used with a verb it is not functioning as a position word, rather, it is indicating a verbal. As a result, 'to write' is not an indirect object but a direct object. It is easier to recognize the verbal in Punjabi since it is a single word ਲਿਖਣਾ likhṇā. Go ahead and complete sentence 2 on the worksheet.

When there is another direct object in the box with the verbal, then its gender reflects that object. For example: "Nick wants to write letters to Sonia" Nick wants what? 'to write letters' (These are both direct objects)

SUBJECT	INDIRECT OBJECT	DIRECT OBJECT	VERB + AUX.VERB
Nick	Sonia to	letters (to write)	wants is
ਨਿਕ	ਸੋਨੀਆ ਨੂੰ	ਚਿੱਠੀਆਂ ਲਿਖਣੀਆਂ	ਚਾਹੁੰਦਾ ਹੈ
Nik	Sonīā nūṇ	ciṭhṭhīāṇ likhṇīāṇ	cāhuṇdā hai

In the example above, "letters" ਚਿੱਠੀਆਂ ciṭhṭhīāṇ is feminine plural, so the verbal ਲਿਖਣਾ likhṇā will also be feminine plural ਲਿਖਣੀਆਂ likhṇīāṇ

NOTE: When there are multiple objects in any of the boxes, then those objects will be in the reverse order from the English order. The reason for this is that in both languages the more direct an object is, the closer it is to the verb. In Punjabi, when the verb moves to the end of the sentence, it brings the direct object with it. In other words, whatever object is closer to the verb in English will also be closer to the verb in Punjabi.

As we learned before, the word 'not' always comes before the main verb. In the following sentence, notice that the word 'not' comes before the main verb 'learn.' Notice, that the above rules for using verbals with the verb 'want' also apply to using verbals with other verbs. For example, "Nick ~~does~~ not learn to write."

SUBJECT	DIRECT OBJECT	VERB + AUX.VERB
Nick	(to write)	not learn is
ਨਿਕ	ਲਿਖਣਾ	ਨਹੀਂ ਸਿੱਖਦਾ ਹੈ
Nik	*likhṇā*	*nahīṇ sikhkhadā hai*

Subjunctive Mood

In 'want' sentences, if the subject wants someone else to carry out some action then the sentence MUST be split into two sentences. These sentences are then joined by the conjunction word 'that' (ਕਿ *ki*)

For example: "Sonia wants me to write" MUST become "Sonia wants that I shall write"

SUBJECT	VERB + AUX.VERB		SUBJECT	VERB
Sonia	wants is	that	I	shall write
ਸੋਨੀਆ	ਚਾਹੁੰਦੀ ਹੈ	ਕਿ	ਮੈਂ	ਲਿਖਾਂ
Sonīā	*cāhuṇdī hai*	*ki*	*maiṇ*	*likhāṇ*

TIP: Always split the English sentence into two sentences before translating.

In compound sentences that use the verb 'want', the verb in the second sentence must use the subjunctive ending "shall/may." The subjunctive ending is used to express a wish or possibility. For example, "I shall write" or "I may write." The subjunctive endings can be formed in one easy step. We will demonstrate how to make the ending for 'I' (ਮੈਂ *maiṇ*).

Step One: Remove the ' ਹ ' from the present tense AUXILIARY VERB (as shown in yellow) and place the remainder behind the ROOT of the verb

ਲਿਖਦਾ ~~ਹ~~ਾਂ = ਲਿਖਾਂ

Notice that the subjunctive ending does not use an auxiliary verb in addition to the ending because THE ENDING IS THE AUXILIARY VERB. Sentences that use the connecting word ਤਾਂਕਿ *tāṇki* (so that) also follow this pattern. The second sentence must use the subjunctive ending "shall/may."

NOTE: Since 'we' and 'I' both use the same auxiliary verb, the subjunctive ending for 'we' is given a unique ending. Also, the ending for the pronoun 'he/she' is slightly modified. Using the "Subjunctive Mood Chart" on page 59, go ahead and complete sentences 3 and 4 on the worksheet.

Verbals as Indirect Objects

Now let's go ahead and use a verbal in the indirect object box. For example: "Nick wants paper for writing". Nick wants what? Nick wants paper. (This is the direct object) Nick wants paper for what? 'for writing' (This is the indirect object because it includes a position word)

SUBJECT	INDIRECT OBJECT	DIRECT OBJECT	VERB + AUX.VERB
Nick	writing for	paper	wants is
ਨਿਕ	ਲਿਖਣ ਲਈ	ਪੇਪਰ	ਚਾਹੁੰਦਾ ਹੈ
Nik	*likhṇ laī*	*pepar*	*cāhuṇdā hai*

Notice in the example above that when a verbal is followed by a position word it also is indirect or oblique. The oblique spelling is formed by omitting the vowel ending. In the example above, the verbal ਲਿਖਣਾ *likhṇā* changes to the oblique ਲਿਖਣ *likhṇ*. Now you can go ahead and complete sentences 5 on the worksheet.

A Method for the Long Term

The daily practice sheet in this lesson contains four exercises. We will divide the fifteen minutes of practice between these four exercises. It is important to spend at least a few minutes on each exercise.

Starting with this lesson, the practice calendar uses a rotating practice schedule. This means that practice sessions will rotate between the completed lessons, with the most recently completed lesson being practiced the most frequently.

As you progress in the course, this method will aid you with long term retention. It has been observed, that as the length of time between practice sessions gradually increases, the strength of the memory increases. In effect, gradually reducing the frequency of practicing something will move it into your long term memory.

When you feel comfortable with performing the daily exercises then you are ready to move on to the next lesson and build larger sentences!

LESSON FOUR VOCABULARY

1. Words with masculine gender are highlighted in blue.
2. Words with feminine gender are highlighted in pink.
3. Words that are used for both the singular and plural form are marked with (s).

bread ਰੋਟੀ *roṭī*	to buy ਖ਼ਰੀਦਣਾ *kharīdṇā*	car ਗੱਡੀ *gaḍḍī*
chair ਕੁਰਸੀ *kursī*	clothes ਕੱਪੜੇ *kappṛe*	easy ਸੌਖਾ *saukhā*
hard ਔਖਾ *aukhā*	house(s) ਘਰ *ghar*	important ਮਹੱਤਵਪੂਰਣ *mahattavpūaṇ*
interesting ਦਿਲਚਸਪ *dilcasp*	money ਪੈਸਾ *paisā*	necessary ਜ਼ਰੂਰੀ *zarūrī*
room ਕਮਰਾ *kamrā*	shoes ਜੁੱਤੀਆਂ *juttīāṇ*	silence ਚੁੱਪ *cupp*
so that ਤਾਂਕਿ *tāṇki*	to want ਚਾਹੁਣਾ *cāhuṇā*	water ਪਾਣੀ *pāṇī*

LESSON FOUR WORKSHEET

Step one: Ask **what is being done?** (Write "V" for verb above the word)
Step two: Ask **who is doing it?** (Write "S" for subject above the word)
Step three: Ask **...what?** (Write "d.O" for direct object above the word)
Step four: Ask **TO what? TO whom?** (Write "i.O" for indirect object above the word)
Step four: Write the English words in the Punjabi word order on the first line
Step five: Write the Punjabi words underneath on the second line.
Step six: Add the appropriate verb ending and auxiliary verb.

1. Learning is important. ______________________________

____

2. We want to listen to you. ______________________________

____

3. I want them to tell. ______________________________

____

4. He shows me so that I might learn. ______________________________

____

5. He wants silence for thinking. ______________________________

____

Vocabulary: am ਹਾਂ | are ਹਨ | for ਲਈ | he ਉਹ | I ਮੈਂ | important ਮਹੱਤਵਪੂਰਣ | is ਹੈ learn ਸਿੱਖਣਾ | to listen ਸੁਣਨਾ | me ਮੈਨੂੰ | to show ਦਿਖਾਉਣਾ | silence ਚੁੱਪ | so that ਤਾਂਕਿ to tell ਦੱਸਣਾ | that ਕਿ | they ਉਹ | to think ਸੋਚਣਾ | to you ਤੁਹਾਨੂੰ | to want ਚਾਹੁਣਾ | we ਅਸੀਂ

SUBJUNCTIVE MOOD CHART

SUBJECT + VERB ROOT + ENDING(AUXILIARY)

Pronoun English	Pronoun Punjabi	Root ending in Consonant	Root ending in Vowel
I	ਮੈਂ	ਬੋਲਾਂ	ANY vowel insert ਵ ਆਵਾਂ
He/She (Singular)	ਉਹ	ਬੋਲੇ	ANY vowel insert ਵ ਆਵੇ
They (Plural)	ਉਹ	ਬੋਲਣ	KANNA ONLY insert ਉ ਆਉਣ Exception: ਜਾਣਾ and ਖਾਣਾ as well as all other vowels use same ending as consonants
We	ਅਸੀਂ	ਬੋਲੀਏ	ANY vowel insert ਏ ਆਈਏ
You	ਤੁਸੀਂ	ਬੋਲੋ	ANY vowel insert ਵ ਆਵੋ

NOTE: If the subject is NOT a pronoun then determine its gender and number. The same endings for (He/She) are used for singular subjects. The same endings for (They) are used for plural subjects.

DAILY PRACTICE SHEET

Instructions for the 'Think and Speak' method:

Do NOT write down the answers – this is the 'think' part

Say each sentence OUT LOUD – this is the 'speak' part

What if I get stuck? Look at the reference charts for help. The goal is NOT to 'memorize' the sentences but to LEARN A METHOD to construct your own sentences.

SUBJECT + I.OBJECT + D.OBJECT + VERB ROOT + ENDING + AUX.VERB

Exercise One: Verbal as Subject

1. Say each sentence OUT LOUD.

1. Eating is important.
ਖਾਣਾ ਮਹੱਤਵਪੂਰਣ ਹੈ
2. Reading is hard.
3. Giving is good.
4. Sleeping is important.
5. Learning is interesting.
6. Singing is easy.
7. Listening is necessary.
8. Driving is hard.

Exercise Two: Verbal as Direct Object

1. Say each sentence OUT LOUD.
2. Add an indirect OR a direct object and repeat the sentence again (When there is another direct object in the box with the verbal, then its gender reflects that object).

1. He wants to ask.
= ਉਹ ਪੁੱਛਣਾ ਚਾਹੁੰਦਾ ਹੈ
2. We want to read.
3. They want to keep.
4. I want to sit.
5. She wants to speak.
6. They want to believe.
7. I want to come.
8. She wants to explain.
9. You want to show.
10. He wants to teach.
11. We want to be.
12. They want to reside/remain.
13. I want to say.
14. She wants to touch.
15. You want to take.
16. He wants to drink.
17. We want to sleep.
18. They want to give.
19. I want to eat.
20. She wants to change.

Exercise Three: Subjunctive Mood (Ending in Vowel)

1. Say each sentence OUT LOUD. (Sentences shaded in gray are exceptions. Check the chart on page 59 for more information)
2. Add an indirect OR a direct object to the SECOND sentence and repeat.

1. We want them to eat.
= ਅਸੀਂ ਚਾਹੁੰਦੇ ਹਾਂ ਕਿ ਉਹ ਖਾਣ
2. He wants us to achieve.
3. They want her to sleep.
4. I want you to bring.
6. You want me to drive.
7. He wants them to explain.
8. We want him to lose.
9. They want us to make.
10. I want you to save/rescue.
11. She wants them to go.
12. You want me to sing.
14. They want him to be.
15. We want them to take.

Exercise Four: Subjunctive Mood (Ending in Consonant)

1. Say each sentence OUT LOUD. (For the sentences shaded in gray, follow the example in sentence two)
2. Add an indirect OR a direct object to the SECOND sentence and repeat.

1. We go so that they **may** reside/remain.
= ਅਸੀਂ ਜਾਂਦੇ ਹਾਂ ਤਾਂਕਿ ਉਹ ਰਹਿਣ
2. We go so that they **can** reside/remain.
(lit. "so that they **may be able** to reside/remain)
= ਅਸੀਂ ਜਾਂਦੇ ਹਾਂ ਤਾਂਕਿ ਉਹ ਰਹਿ ਸਕਣ
3. They meet so that they may become.
5. I call so that you may come out.
6. We learn so that we can understand.
7. She tells so that I may know.
8. He sings so that she can listen.
9. We come so that we may meet.
10. They call so that he may open.
11. I save so that I can buy.
12. She sits so that they may see.
13. He walks so that he may think.
14. You lose so that we may find.
15. They teach so that you can write.
16. I come out so that I may walk.

PRACTICE CALENDAR

Box 1: Practice 5 minutes or more of exercises **one & two** and then ✓ check box 1

Box 2: Practice 5 minutes or more of exercise **three** and then ✓ check box 2

Box 3: Practice 5 minutes or more of exercise **four** and then ✓ check box 3

Review Day: Practice lesson three exercises on pages 48-49.

	Week 1			Week 2			Week 3			Week 4		
Monday	1	2	3	1	2	3	1	2	3	1	2	3
Tuesday	1	2	3	1	2	3	1	2	3	1	2	3
Wednesday	1	2	3	1	2	3	1	2	3	1	2	3
Thursday	1	2	3	1	2	3	1	2	3	1	2	3
Friday	1	2	3	1	2	3	1	2	3	1	2	3
Saturday	1	2	3	1	2	3	1	2	3	1	2	3
Sunday	1	2	3	1	2	3	1	2	3	1	2	3

WORKSHEET ANSWERS

Step one: Ask **what is being done?** (Write "V" for verb above the word)
Step two: Ask **who is doing it?** (Write "S" for subject above the word)
Step three: Ask **...what?** (Write "d.O" for direct object above the word)
Step four: Ask **TO what? TO whom?** (Write "i.O" for indirect object above the word)
Step four: Write the English words in the Punjabi word order on the first line
Step five: Write the Punjabi words underneath on the second line.
Step six: Add the appropriate verb ending and auxiliary verb.

1. Learning is important.
Learning important is
ਸਿੱਖਣਾ ਮਹੱਤਵਪੂਰਣ ਹੈ

2. We want (to listen) to you.
We to you (to listen) want
ਅਸੀਂ ਤੁਹਾਨੂੰ ਸੁਣਨਾ ਚਾਹੁੰਦੇ ਹਾਂ

3. I want them to tell.
Reword: I want that they shall tell.
I want that they (shall tell)
ਮੈਂ ਚਾਹੁੰਦੀ ਹਾਂ ਕਿ ਉਹ ਦੱਸਣ
ਮੈਂ ਚਾਹੁੰਦਾ ਹਾਂ ਕਿ ਉਹ ਦੱਸਣ

4. He shows me so that I can learn.
Reword: He shows me so that I might learn.
He me shows so that I (might learn)
ਉਹ ਮੈਨੂੰ ਦਿਖਾਉਂਦਾ ਹੈ ਤਾਂਕਿ ਮੈਂ ਸਿੱਖਾਂ

5. He wants silence (for thinking.)
He thinking for silence wants
ਉਹ ਸੋਚਣ ਲਈ ਚੁੱਪ ਚਾਹੁੰਦਾ ਹੈ

Vocabulary: am ਹਾਂ | are ਹਨ | for ਲਈ | he ਉਹ | I ਮੈਂ | important ਮਹੱਤਵਪੂਰਣ | is ਹੈ | learn ਸਿੱਖਣਾ | to listen ਸੁਣਨਾ | me ਮੈਨੂੰ | to show ਦਿਖਾਉਣਾ | silence ਚੁੱਪ | so that ਤਾਂਕਿ | to tell ਦੱਸਣਾ | that ਕਿ | they ਉਹ | to think ਸੋਚਣਾ | to you ਤੁਹਾਨੂੰ | to want ਚਾਹੁਣਾ | we ਅਸੀਂ

PASSIVE AND FUTURE

Future Tense

The future tense endings are very similar to the subjunctive endings that we learned in lesson four. We can use the same method with just one extra step. We will demonstrate how to make the ending for 'I' (ਮੈਂ *maiṇ*).

Step One: Remove the 'ਹ' from the present tense AUXILIARY VERB (as shown in yellow) and place the remainder behind the ROOT of the verb

ਲਿਖਦਾ ਹਾਂ = ਲਿਖਾਂ

Step Two: Replace the 'ਦ' from the present tense ENDING with 'ਗ' and place this at the end of the verb (as shown in red)

ਲਿਖਦਾ ਹਾਂ = ਲਿਖਾਂਗਾ

Notice that the future tense ending combines the auxiliary verb with the ending.

NOTE: The ending for the pronoun 'he/she' is slightly modified. Find page 70 entitled "Lesson Five Worksheet." Using the "Future Tense Chart – Verb Roots Ending with Consonants" on page 71 and the "Future Tense Chart – Verb Roots Ending with Vowels" on page 72, go ahead and translate sentences 1 and 2.

Passive Sentences

Up to this point, we have been using active sentences like "Nick writes the letter." The same sentence in the passive voice would be: "The letter is written by Nick." The passive voice is used to place more emphasis on the action and less importance on the person who performs that action.

Strong Obligation

In Punjabi, sentences that express strong obligation can ONLY be expressed in the passive voice. The emphasis must be placed on the action and not on the person who is performing that action.

For example, in Punjabi, you cannot say "Nick should write the letter" which is in the active voice. Instead, you MUST use the passive voice: "The letter should be written by Nick." The following verbs must always be used in the passive voice:

ਚਾਹੀਦਾ *cāhīdā* (Should/Ought) is used to express a responsibility or sense of duty
 e.g. "I ought to work.

ਪੈਂਦਾ *paiṇdā* (Have/Must) is used to express a compelling force or pressure
 e.g. "I have to breathe."

With these sentences, the passive voice is formed simply by adding the postposition ਨੂੰ *nūṇ* to the subject. For example: "Nick ought to write"

SUBJECT	DIRECT OBJECT	VERB + AUX.VERB
Nick	to write	ought is
ਨਿਕ ਨੂੰ	ਲਿਖਣਾ	ਚਾਹੀਦਾ ਹੈ
Nik nūṇ	*likhṇā*	*cāhīdā hai*

Tip! Remember to use the charts on page 31 and 32 when using the postposition ਨੂੰ with pronouns and masculine nouns.

Notice how the postposition changes the spelling of the pronoun in the next sentence, “We have to write”

SUBJECT	DIRECT OBJECT	VERB + AUX.VERB
We	to write	have is
ਸਾਨੂੰ	ਲਿਖਣਾ	ਪੈਂਦਾ ਹੈ
sānūṇ	*likhṇā*	*paiṇdā hai*

Notice, we cannot say “to we” (ਅਸੀਂ ਨੂੰ *āsīṇ nūṇ*) Instead, we must use the oblique spelling “to us” (ਸਾਨੂੰ *sānūṇ*)

In review, you will notice that using ‘should’ or ‘have to’ sentences is the same as using ‘want’ sentences, except that we need to add the postposition ਨੂੰ *nūṇ* to the subject. We have learned that postpositions affect the spelling of the nouns that they follow. Now we will learn another property of postpositions. Postpositions also cancel the gender of the nouns that they follow.

To review: 1. Postpositions affect spelling

2. Postpositions cancel gender

This second property becomes very important when using sentences that express obligation. In the sentence “She has to write” notice that the postposition cancels the gender of the subject. As a result, both the verb and the auxiliary verb take the default gender. In Punjabi, the default gender is the masculine singular form.

SUBJECT	DIRECT OBJECT	VERB + AUX.VERB
She	to write	has is
ਉਸ ਨੂੰ	ਲਿਖਣਾ	ਪੈਂਦਾ ਹੈ
us nūṇ	*likhṇā*	*paiṇdā hai*

The next sentence "Nick will have to write ~~a~~ letter" shows that if there is an object in the sentence, the verb and the auxiliary verb will agree with the gender and number of the object. The word 'letter' is feminine singular so we will use the feminine singular ending.

SUBJECT	DIRECT OBJECT	VERB
Nick	letter (to write)	will have
ਨਿਕ ਨੂੰ	ਚਿੱਠੀ ਲਿਖਣੀ	ਪਵੇਗੀ
Nik nūṇ	*ciṭhṭhī likhṇī*	*pavegī*

TIP: When adding the postposition ਨੂੰ *nūṇ* to the subject, the verb will take the default masculine singular gender unless there is an object in the sentence. Go ahead and translate sentences 3 – 5 on the worksheet.

Time of Day

To state the time in English, we often use the word *o'clock* (lit. according to the clock) For example, "It is one o'clock." (lit. "It is one according to the clock")

In Punjabi, we use the word 'chime' (ਵਜਾ *vajā*)For example, "It is one o'clock." ਇਕ ਵਜਾ ਹੈ *ik vajā hai* (lit. one chime is) or "It is two o'clock." ਦੋ ਵਜੇ ਹਨ *do vaje han* (lit. two chimes are) We can easily add the time of day to any sentence.

For example, "We will read until one o'clock"

SUBJECT	INDIRECT OBJECT	VERB + AUX.VERB
We	one o'clock until	will read
ਅਸੀਂ	ਇਕ ਵਜੇ ਤਕ	ਪੜ੍ਹਾਂਗੇ
āsīṇ	*ik vaje tak*	*paṛhāṇge*

Or we can say, "We will eat at one o'clock"

SUBJECT	INDIRECT OBJECT	VERB + AUX.VERB
We	one o'clock at	will eat
ਅਸੀਂ	ਇਕ ਵਜੇ	ਖਾਵਾਂਗੇ
āsīṇ	*ik vaje*	*khāvāṇge*

Notice that the position word 'at' is understood to be included, but is not written or spoken. It is for this reason that ਵਜਾ *vajā* is still in the oblique form ਵਜੇ *vaje*

Future Tense Irregular Verbs

There are a handful of verbs that follow an irregular construction in the future tense. These can be found in the reference chart "Irregular Verbs - Future Tense" on page 73.

The daily practice sheet in this lesson contains four exercises. We will divide the fifteen minutes of practice between these four exercises. It is important to spend at least a few minutes on each exercise.

The practice calendar continues to use a rotating practice schedule. This means that practice sessions will rotate between the completed lessons, with the most recently completed lesson being practiced the most frequently.

When you feel comfortable with performing the daily exercises then you are ready to move on to the next lesson and build larger sentences!

LESSON FIVE VOCABULARY

1. Words with masculine gender are highlighted in blue.
2. Words with feminine gender are highlighted in pink.
3. Words that are used for both the singular and plural form are marked with (s).

chimes/o'clock ਵਜੇ *vaje*	have/must to fall (rain or snow) ਪੈਣਾ *paiṇā*	rain ਮੀਂਹ *mīṇh*
should/ought ਚਾਹੀਦਾ *cāhīdā*	snow/ice ਬਰਫ਼ *barf*	until/up to ਤਕ *tak*
one ਇਕ *ik*	two ਦੋ *do*	three ਤਿੰਨ *tiṇn*
four ਚਾਰ *cār*	five ਪੰਜ *paṇj*	six ਛੇ *che*
seven ਸੱਤ *satt*	eight ਅੱਠ *āṭhṭh*	nine ਨੌਂ *nauṇ*
ten ਦਸ *das*	eleven ਗਿਆਰਾਂ *giārāṇ*	twelve ਬਾਰ੍ਹਾਂ *bārhāṇ*

LESSON FIVE WORKSHEET

Step one: Ask **what is being done?** (Write "V" for verb above the word)
Step two: Ask **who is doing it?** (Write "S" for subject above the word)
Step three: Ask **...what?** (Write "d.O" for direct object above the word)
Step four: Ask **TO what? TO whom?** (Write "i.O" for indirect object above the word)
Step four: Write the English words in the Punjabi word order on the first line
Step five: Write the Punjabi words underneath on the second line.
Step six: Add the appropriate verb ending and auxiliary verb.

1. We will listen. ______________________________

____

2. You will go. ______________________________

____

3. She has to eat. ______________________________

____

4. They have to read the book. ______________________________

____

5. I should/ought to meet with him. ______________________________

____

Vocabulary: book ਕਿਤਾਬ (feminine) | to go ਜਾਣਾ | to eat ਖਾਣਾ | have/must ਪੈਣਾ
he/she ਉਹ | I ਮੈਂ | is ਹੈ | to listen ਸੁਣਨਾ | to meet ਮਿਲਣਾ | to read ਪੜ੍ਹਨਾ
should/ought ਚਾਹੀਦਾ | they ਉਹ | we ਅਸੀਂ | with ਨਾਲ | you ਤੁਸੀਂ

FUTURE TENSE CHART

VERB ROOTS ENDING WITH CONSONANTS

SUBJECT + VERB ROOT + AUX.VERB + ENDING

Pronoun English	Pronoun Punjabi	Masculine Endings	Feminine Endings
I	ਮੈਂ	ਬੋਲਾਂਗਾ	ਬੋਲਾਂਗੀ
He/She (Singular)	ਉਹ	ਬੋਲੇਗਾ	ਬੋਲੇਗੀ
They (Plural)	ਉਹ	ਬੋਲਣਗੇ	ਬੋਲਣਗੀਆਂ
We	ਅਸੀਂ	ਬੋਲਾਂਗੇ	
You	ਤੁਸੀਂ	ਬੋਲੋਗੇ	

NOTE: If the subject is NOT a pronoun then determine its gender and number. The same endings for (He/She) are used for singular subjects. The same endings for (They) are used for plural subjects.

FUTURE TENSE CHART

VERB ROOTS ENDING WITH OTHER VOWELS

SUBJECT + VERB ROOT + AUX.VERB + ENDING

<table>
<tr><th>Pronoun English</th><th>Pronoun Punjabi</th><th>Masculine Endings</th><th>Feminine Endings</th></tr>
<tr><td>I</td><td>ਮੈਂ</td><td>If root ends in ANY vowel insert ਵ
ਆਵਾਂਗਾ</td><td>If root ends in ANY vowel insert ਵ
ਆਵਾਂਗੀ</td></tr>
<tr><td>He/She (Singular)</td><td>ਉਹ</td><td>If root ends in ANY vowel insert ਵ
ਆਵੇਗਾ</td><td>If root ends in ANY vowel insert ਵ
ਆਵੇਗੀ</td></tr>
<tr><td>They (Plural)</td><td>ਉਹ</td><td>KANNA ONLY insert ਉ
ਆਉਣਗੇ
Exception: ਜਾਣਾ and ਖਾਣਾ as well as all other vowels use same ending as consonants</td><td>KANNA ONLY insert ਉ
ਆਉਣਗੀਆਂ
Exception: ਜਾਣਾ and ਖਾਣਾ as well as all other vowels use same ending as consonants</td></tr>
<tr><td>We</td><td>ਅਸੀਂ</td><td colspan="2">If root ends in ANY vowel insert ਵ
ਆਵਾਂਗੇ</td></tr>
<tr><td>You</td><td>ਤੁਸੀਂ</td><td colspan="2">If root ends in ANY vowel insert ਓ
Exception: ਹੋਣਾ and ਦੇਣਾ insert ਵ and use same ending as consonants
ਆਓਗੇ</td></tr>
</table>

IRREGULAR VERBS - FUTURE TENSE

Remove vowel from root	They (Plural) Use full root
to say ਕਹਿਣਾ ਕਹਾਂਗਾ/ਗੀ ਕਹੇਗਾ/ਗੀ ਕਹਾਂਗੇ ਕਹੋਗੇ I He/She We You	ਕਹਿਣਗੇ/ਗੀਆਂ They
to reside/to remain ਰਹਿਣਾ ਰਹਾਂਗਾ/ਗੀ ਰਹੇਗਾ/ਗੀ ਰਹਾਂਗੇ ਰਹੋਗੇ I He/She We You	ਰਹਿਣਗੇ/ਗੀਆਂ They
to want ਚਾਹੁਣਾ ਚਾਹਾਂਗਾ/ਗੀ ਚਾਹੇਗਾ/ਗੀ ਚਾਹਾਂਗੇ ਚਾਹੋਗੇ I He/She We You	ਚਾਹੁਣਗੇ/ਗੀਆਂ They
Remove vowel from root and insert ਵ	They (Plural) Use full root
to take ਲੈਣਾ ਲਵਾਂਗਾ/ਗੀ ਲਵੇਗਾ/ਗੀ ਲਵਾਂਗੇ ਲਵੋਗੇ I He/She We You	ਲੈਣਗੇ/ਗੀਆ They
to have (obligation) ਪੈਣਾ ਪਵਾਂਗਾ/ਗੀ ਪਵੇਗਾ/ਗੀ ਪਵਾਂਗੇ ਪਵੋਗੇ I He/She We You	ਪੈਣਗੇ/ਗੀਆਂ They

DAILY PRACTICE SHEET

Instructions for the 'Think and Speak' method:

Do NOT write down the answers – this is the 'think' part

Say each sentence OUT LOUD – this is the 'speak' part

What if I get stuck? Look at the reference charts for help. The goal is NOT to 'memorize' the sentences but to LEARN A METHOD to construct your own sentences.

SUBJECT + I.OBJECT + D.OBJECT + VERB ROOT + AUX.VERB + ENDING

Exercise One: Future Tense (Roots Ending in Consonants)

Say each sentence OUT LOUD.

1. He will ask.
= ਉਹ ਪੁੱਛੇਗਾ
2. We will become.
3. They will believe/accept.
4. I will change.
5. She will emerge/come out.
6. You will find.
7. He will know.
8. We will learn.
9. They will listen/hear.
10. I will meet.
11. She will open.
12. You will put/keep.
13. He will read.
14. We will see.
15. They will touch.
16. I will sit.
17. She will talk/speak.
18. You will tell.
19. He will think.
20. We will understand.
21. They will walk.
22. I will write.
23. She will ask.

Exercise Two: Irregular Verbs

Say each sentence OUT LOUD.

1. He will say.
= ਉਹ ਕਹੇਗਾ
2. We will remain.
3. They will want.
4. I will take.
5. She will have.
6. You will say.
7. He will remain.
8. We will want.
9. They will take.
10. I will have.
11. She will say.

Exercise Three: Future Tense (Roots Ending in Vowels)

Say each sentence OUT LOUD.

1. We will achieve/wear.
= ਅਸੀਂ ਪਾਵਾਂਗੇ
2. We will bring.
3. They will call.
4. I will come.
5. She will drive.
6. You will explain.
7. He will lose.
8. We will make.
9. They will save.
10. I will show.
11. She will sing.
12. You will teach.
13. He put on/wear.
14. We will take.
15. They will drink.
16. I will sleep.
17. She will go.
18. You will eat.
19. He will give.
20. We will be/happen.

Exercise Four: Strong Obligation

1. Say each sentence OUT LOUD.
2. Add an indirect OR a direct object and repeat the sentence again.

1. She should/ought to ask.
= ਉਸ ਨੂੰ ਪੁੱਛਣਾ ਚਾਹੀਦਾ ਹੈ
2. We should/ought to change.
3. They should/ought to know.
4. I should/ought to learn.
5. She should/ought to listen.
6. You should/ought to read.
7. He should/ought to see.
8. We should/ought to sit.
9. They should/ought to speak.
10. I should/ought to tell.
11. She should/ought to think.
12. He has to ask.
= ਉਸ ਨੂੰ ਪੁੱਛਣਾ ਪੈਂਦਾ ਹੈ
13. You have to understand.
14. He has to walk.
15. We have to write.
16. They have to come.
17. I have to drive.
18. She has to sing.
19. You have to explain.
20. He has to show.
21. We have to teach.
22. They have to take.

PRACTICE CALENDAR

Box 1: Practice 5 minutes or more of exercise one and then ✓ check box 1

Box 2: Practice 5 minutes or more of exercises two & three and then ✓ check box 2

Box 3: Practice 5 minutes or more of exercise four and then ✓ check box 3

Review Day: Practice lesson four exercises on pages 60-61.

Review Day: Practice lesson three exercises on pages 48-49.

	Week 1			Week 2			Week 3			Week 4		
Monday	1	2	3	1	2	3	1	2	3	1	2	3
Tuesday	1	2	3	1	2	3	1	2	3	1	2	3
Wednesday	1	2	3	1	2	3	1	2	3	1	2	3
Thursday	1	2	3	1	2	3	1	2	3	1	2	3
Friday	1	2	3	1	2	3	1	2	3	1	2	3
Saturday	1	2	3	1	2	3	1	2	3	1	2	3
Sunday	1	2	3	1	2	3	1	2	3	1	2	3

WORKSHEET ANSWERS

Step one: Ask **what is being done?** (Write "V" for verb above the word)
Step two: Ask **who is doing it?** (Write "S" for subject above the word)
Step three: Ask **...what?** (Write "d.O" for direct object above the word)
Step four: Ask **TO what? TO whom?** (Write "i.O" for indirect object above the word)
Step four: Write the English words in the Punjabi word order on the first line
Step five: Write the Punjabi words underneath on the second line.
Step six: Add the appropriate verb ending and auxiliary verb.

1. We (will listen).

We will listen

ਅਸੀਂ ਸੁਣਾਂਗੇ

2. You (will go).

You will go

ਤੁਸੀਂ ਜਾਓਗੇ

3. She has (to eat).

She to eat has

ਉਸ ਨੂੰ ਖਾਣਾ ਪੈਂਦਾ ਹੈ

4. They have (to read the book).

They book to read have

ਉਹਨਾਂ ਨੂੰ ਕਿਤਾਬ ਪੜ੍ਹਨੀ ਪੈਂਦੀ ਹੈ

5. I should/ought (to meet) (with him).

I him with to meet should

ਮੈਨੂੰ ਉਸ ਨਾਲ ਮਿਲਣਾ ਚਾਹੀਦਾ ਹੈ

Vocabulary: book ਕਿਤਾਬ (feminine) | to go ਜਾਣਾ | to eat ਖਾਣਾ | have ਪੈਂਦਾ
he/she ਉਹ | I ਮੈਂ | is ਹੈ | to listen ਸੁਣਨਾ | to meet ਮਿਲਣਾ | to read ਪੜ੍ਹਨਾ
should/ought ਚਾਹੀਦਾ | they ਉਹ | we ਅਸੀਂ | with ਨਾਲ | you ਤੁਸੀਂ

PAST TENSE AND ADJECTIVES

Past Tense

The past tense endings are based on the present tense endings that we learned in lesson one. As with the present tense, there are four different past tense endings (1)masculine singular (2)masculine plural (3)feminine singular and (4) feminine plural. The past tense endings can be formed in two easy steps. We will demonstrate how to make the masculine PLURAL ending.

Step One: Remove the ' ਦ ' from the present tense ENDING (as shown in red)and place the remainder behind the ROOT of the verb

ਲਿਖ~~ਦੇ~~ ਹਨ = ਲਿਖੇ

Step Two: Replace the ' ਹ ' from the AUXILIARY VERB with ' ਸ ' and place this after the verb (as shown in yellow)

ਲਿਖਦੇ ਹਨ = ਲਿਖੇ ਸਨ

Exceptions: The masculine singular ending inserts an extra vowel sound between the verb root and the ending. Otherwise, the ending would sound like the subjunctive ending for 'I' (ਮੈਂ *maiṇ*). Also, the SINGULAR form of the auxiliary verb is slightly modified.

> Singular subjects use the auxiliary verb ਸੀ *sī*
> Plural subjects use the auxiliary verb ਸਨ *san*

See the "Past Tense Chart – Verb Roots Ending in Consonants" and the "Past Tense Chart – Verb Roots Ending in Vowels" on pages 86-87 for the different endings and auxiliary verbs in the past tense.

A Special Postposition

In Punjabi, there is a special postposition that is used only in the past tense. This postposition has no equivalent in English. This special postposition ਨੇ *ne* is used with the subject. Like all other postpositions, ਨੇ *ne* cancels the gender of the word before it. As a result, the verb will take the default gender unless there is an object in the sentence. For example: "Nick sent a letter to Sonia"

SUBJECT	INDIRECT OBJECT	DIRECT OBJECT	VERB + AUX.VERB
Nick	Sonia to	a letter	sent was
ਨਿਕ ਨੇ	ਸੋਨੀਆ ਨੂੰ	ਚਿੱਠੀ	ਭੇਜੀ ਸੀ
Nik ne	*Sonīā nūṇ*	*ciṭhṭhī*	*bhejī sī*

TIP! With the pronouns ਮੈਂ *maiṇ*, ਤੁਸੀਂ *tusīṇ* and ਅਸੀਂ *āsīṇ* the postposition ਨੇ *ne* is understood to be included, but is not written or spoken.

Present, Remote & Habitual Past

Sentences in the past tense are formed according to whether:

1. an action occurred in the **present past** (use ਨੇ *ne*)
2. an action occurred in the **remote past** (use ਨੇ *ne*)
3. an action occurred regularly or **habitually** in the **past**

Scenario 1: Nick is on the phone to Sonia. As he drops the mail into the post office box she tells her mother, "He sent the letter." ਉਸ ਨੇ ਚਿੱਠੀ ਭੇਜੀ *us ne ciṭhṭhī bhejī*

Scenario 2: Nick sends a letter to Sonia. Two weeks later, she tells a friend, "He sent the letter" ਉਸ ਨੇ ਚਿੱਠੀ ਭੇਜੀ ਸੀ *us ne ciṭhṭhī bhejī sī*

Scenario 3: Nick no longer sends letters to Sonia. She tells a friend, "He **used to** send letters." ਉਹ ਚਿੱਠੀਆਂ ਭੇਜਦਾ ਸੀ *uh ciṭhṭhīāṇ bhejdā sī* or ਉਹ ਚਿੱਠੀਆਂ ਭੇਜਦਾ ਹੁੰਦਾ ਸੀ *uh ciṭhṭhīāṇ bhejdā huṇdā sī*.

Notice in scenario three that the habitual past does NOT use the postposition ਨੇ *ne*. As a result, the gender of the subject is not canceled and the verb agrees with the subject.

NOTE: The past tense of "to know" ਜਾਣਿਆ *jāṇiā* is rarely used. Instead, it is common to express "knew" in the habitual past as ਜਾਣਦਾ ਸੀ *jāṇdā sī*. For example, "He knew the answer" would be ਉਹ ਜਵਾਬ ਜਾਣਦਾ ਸੀ *uh javāb jāṇdā sī*

Putting Theory into Practice

At this point, find page 85 entitled "Lesson Six Worksheet" and complete sentences 1 – 3.

Strong Obligation - in The Past Tense

In lesson five we learned about strong obligation. With a past tense sentence that expresses strong obligation, we do not use both ਨੂੰ *nūṇ* and ਨੇ *ne* behind the subject. Instead, we use only ਨੂੰ *nūṇ.* For example: "Sonia had to go"

SUBJECT	DIRECT OBJECT	VERB + AUX.VERB
Sonia	to go	had was
ਸੋਨੀਆ ਨੂੰ	ਜਾਣਾ	ਪਿਆ ਸੀ
Sonīā nūṇ	*jāṇā*	*piā sī*

Ability - In the Past Tense

In lesson three we learned about the verb ਸਕਣਾ *sakṇā* (to be able/can). This verb does not use the postposition ਨੇ *ne* in the past tense. For example, "Sonia could not go." (lit. "Sonia was not able to go.")

SUBJECT	VERB + AUX.VERB
Sonia	not go could was
ਸੋਨੀਆ	ਨਹੀਂ ਜਾ ਸਕੀ ਸੀ
Sonīā	*nahīṇ jā sakī sī*

A very limited number of verbs, and only under certain circumstances, do not use the postposition ਨੇ *ne*. These exceptions can be learned through observation.

Adjectives

An adjective is a word that gives descriptive information about a NOUN. Similar to English, the adjective comes before the noun. In Punjabi, there are two types of adjectives, variable and invariable.

1. Variable adjectives change their endings to reflect the gender and number of the noun that they are describing. Variable adjectives are easy to identify because they end in either ਾ for the masculine or ੀ for the feminine.
2. Invariable adjectives do not change. They also are easy to identify because they do not end with either ਾ or ੀ

Notice in the following two examples how the variable adjective ਸੋਹਣਾ *sohṇā* (beautiful) changes to match the object that it is describing.

For example, in the sentence "Nick writes a beautiful letter" the object 'letter' is feminine singular.

SUBJECT	OBJECT	VERB + AUX.VERB
Nick	beautiful letter	writes is
ਨਿਕ	ਸੋਹਣੀ ਚਿੱਠੀ	ਲਿਖਦਾ ਹੈ
Nik	*sohṇī ciṭhṭhī*	*likhdā hai*

Whereas, in the sentence "Nick writes beautiful letters" the object 'letters' is feminine plural.

SUBJECT	OBJECT	VERB + AUX.VERB
Nick	beautiful letters	writes is
ਨਿਕ	ਸੋਹਣੀਆਂ ਚਿੱਠੀਆਂ	ਲਿਖਦਾ ਹੈ
Nik	*sohṇīāṇ ciṭhṭhīāṇ*	*likhdā hai*

Possessive Adjectives

Possessive adjectives include the words: my, our, your, his, her & their. In Punjabi, these adjectives are variable and change to match the object being possessed.

For example, both men and women would say " ਮੇਰਾ ਨਾਮ" *merā nām* because ਨਾਮ *nām* (name) is a masculine noun and the possessive adjective changes according to the object being possessed and not according to the possessor.

The Apostrophe

In English, the apostrophe with an 's' is often used to show possession. For example, we can say "I received Nick's letter." However, this phrase can also be written out in full as "the letter of Nick" In Punjabi, there is no apostrophe so the phrase must be written out in full. Since 'of' (ਦਾ *dā*) is a postposition in Punjabi, "~~the~~ letter of Nick" would become "Nick of letter" or ਨਿਕ ਦੀ ਚਿੱਠੀ *Nik dī ciṭhṭhī*

Like possessive adjectives, the possessive postposition ਦਾ *dā* also agrees with the object being possessed and not the possessor. In the example below, notice that ਦੀ *dī* becomes ਦੀਆਂ *dīāṇ* when we change letter to letters. "Nick of letters" or ਨਿਕ ਦੀਆਂ ਚਿੱਠੀਆਂ *Nik dīāṇ ciṭhṭhīṇ* Go ahead and complete sentences 4 & 5.

Past Tense Irregular Verbs

There are a handful of verbs that follow an irregular construction in the past tense. These can be found in the reference chart "Irregular Verbs - Past Tense" on pages 88-89.

The daily practice sheet in this lesson contains four exercises. We will divide the fifteen minutes of practice between these four exercises. It is important to spend at least a few minutes on each exercise.

The practice calendar continues to use a rotating practice schedule. When you feel comfortable with performing the daily exercises then you are ready to move on to the next lesson and build larger sentences!

LESSON SIX VOCABULARY

1. Variable adjectives change their endings to reflect the gender and number of the noun that they are describing.
2. Invariable adjectives do not change and are marked as (Invariable).

all ਸਾਰਾ sārā	bad ਬੁਰਾ burā	beautiful ਸੋਹਣਾ sohṇā
big ਵੱਡਾ vaḍḍā	different ਵੱਖਰਾ vakhkharā	fat ਮੋਟਾ moṭā
first ਪਹਿਲਾ pahilā	his/her ਉਸ ਦਾ us dā	long/tall ਲੰਬਾ lanbā
new ਨਵਾਂ navāṇ	next ਅਗਲਾ aglā	old ਪੁਰਾਣਾ purāṇā
other/second ਦੂਜਾ dūjā	other/second ਦੂਸਰਾ dūsrā	small/short ਛੋਟਾ choṭā
their ਉਹਨਾਂ ਦਾ uhnāṇ dā	tiny/little ਥੋੜ੍ਹਾ thoṛhā	very (Invariable) ਬਹੁਤ bahut

LESSON SIX WORKSHEET

Step one: Ask **what is being done?** (Write "V" for verb above the word)
Step two: Ask **who is doing it?** (Write "S" for subject above the word)
Step three: Ask **...what?** (Write "d.O" for direct object above the word)
Step four: Ask **TO what? TO whom?** (Write "i.O" for indirect object above the word)
Step four: Write the English words in the Punjabi word order on the first line
Step five: Write the Punjabi words underneath on the second line.
Step six: Add the appropriate verb ending and auxiliary verb.

1. He read the book.
(present past) ______________________________

____

2. They saw the movie.
(remote past) ______________________________

____

3. He used to live in India.
(habitual past) ______________________________

____

4. We wrote a short letter.
(remote past) ______________________________

____

5. She told them your name.
(present past) ______________________________

____

Vocabulary: book ਕਿਤਾਬ (feminine) | he/she ਉਹ | in ਵਿੱਚ | India ਭਾਰਤ | letter ਚਿੱਠੀ (feminine) | to live ਰਹਿਣਾ | movie ਫਿਲਮ (feminine) | name ਨਾਮ (masculine)
to read ਪੜ੍ਹਨਾ | to see ਦੇਖਣਾ | short ਛੋਟਾ | to tell ਦੱਸਣਾ | they ਉਹ | to ਨੂੰ | was ਸੀ | we ਅਸੀਂ
to write ਲਿਖਣਾ | your ਤੁਹਾਡਾ

PAST TENSE CHART
VERB ROOTS ENDING WITH CONSONANTS

SUBJECT + ਨੇ + VERB ROOT + ENDING + AUX.VERB

	Masculine Endings	Feminine Endings	Aux.Verb
Singular	ਬੋਲਿਆ	ਬੋਲੀ	ਸੀ
Plural	ਬੋਲੇ	ਬੋਲੀਆਂ	ਸਨ

In the present past and remote past tenses, the postposition ਨੇ cancels the gender of the subject. As a result, the verb must agree with the OBJECT. Determine the gender and number of the object and use the endings above. If there is no object in the sentence, use the default masculine singular ending.

The habitual past tense does NOT use the postposition ਨੇ *ne*. As a result, the gender of the subject is not canceled and the verb agrees with the subject. If the subject is a pronoun, use the auxiliary verb as shown below.

ਮੈਂ I	ਉਹ he/she	ਅਸੀਂ we	ਤੁਸੀਂ you	ਉਹ they
ਸੀ				ਸਨ

PAST TENSE CHART

VERB ROOTS ENDING WITH VOWELS

SUBJECT + ਨੇ + VERB ROOT + ENDING + AUX.VERB

	Masculine Endings	Feminine Endings	Aux.Verb
Singular	ਆਇਆ (if root ends in ANY vowel insert ੲ)	ਆਈ (if root ends in ANY vowel insert ੲ)	ਸੀ
Plural	ਆਏ (if root ends in ANY vowel insert ੲ)	ਆਈਆਂ (if root ends in ANY vowel insert ੲ)	ਸਨ

In the present past and remote past tenses, the postposition ਨੇ cancels the gender of the subject. As a result, the verb must agree with the OBJECT. Determine the gender and number of the object and use the endings above. If there is no object in the sentence, use the default masculine singular ending.

The habitual past tense does NOT use the postposition ਨੇ *ne*. As a result, the gender of the subject is not canceled and the verb agrees with the subject. If the subject is a pronoun, use the auxiliary verb as shown below.

ਮੈਂ I	ਉਹ he/she	ਅਸੀਂ we	ਤੁਸੀਂ you	ਉਹ they
ਸੀ				ਸਨ

IRREGULAR VERBS – PAST TENSE

Remove vowel from root	
to want/wish ਚਾਹੁਣਾ ਚਾਹਿਆ ਚਾਹੀ ਚਾਹੇ ਚਾਹੀਆਂ m/s f/s m/p f/p	to take ਲੈਣਾ ਲਿਆ ਲਈ ਲਏ ਲਈਆਂ m/s f/s m/p f/p
Remove vowel from root and subject takes the position word ਨੂੰ instead of ਨੇ	Remove vowel from root and use ਗ instead of ਜ
to have (obligation) ਪੈਣਾ ਪਿਆ ਪਈ ਪਏ ਪਈਆਂ m/s f/s m/p f/p	to go ਜਾਣਾ ਗਿਆ ਗਈ ਗਏ ਗਈਆਂ m/s f/s m/p f/p

The following verbs use an abbreviated masculine singular ending	
Insert ਤ before ending	Insert ਧ before ending
to drink ਪੀਣਾ ਪੀਤਾ ਪੀਤੀ ਪੀਤੇ ਪੀਤੀਆਂ m/s f/s m/p f/p	to eat ਖਾਣਾ ਖਾਧਾ ਖਾਧੀ ਖਾਧੇ ਖਾਧੀਆਂ m/s f/s m/p f/p

IRREGULAR VERBS - PAST TENSE

The following verb use an abbreviated masculine singular ending (cont.)

Replace vowel and insert ੱਤ before ending

to sleep ਸੌਣਾ			
ਸੁੱਤਾ	ਸੁੱਤੀ	ਸੁੱਤੇ	ਸੁੱਤੀਆਂ
m/s	f/s	m/p	f/p

to give ਦੇਣਾ			
ਦਿੱਤਾ	ਦਿੱਤੀ	ਦਿੱਤੇ	ਦਿੱਤੀਆਂ
m/s	f/s	m/p	f/p

Remove ਰ from root and insert ੀਤ before ending

to do ਕਰਨਾ			
ਕੀਤਾ	ਕੀਤੀ	ਕੀਤੇ	ਕੀਤੀਆਂ
m/s	f/s	m/p	f/p

Remove the vowel (For masculine singular, move the vowel infront of the root)

to say ਕਹਿਣਾ			
ਕਿਹਾ	ਕਹੀ	ਕਹੇ	ਕਹੀਆਂ
m/s	f/s	m/p	f/p

to reside/remain ਰਹਿਣਾ			
ਰਿਹਾ	ਰਹੀ	ਰਹੇ	ਰਹੀਆਂ
m/s	f/s	m/p	f/p

GENDER REVIEW

1. The VERB agrees with the SUBJECT

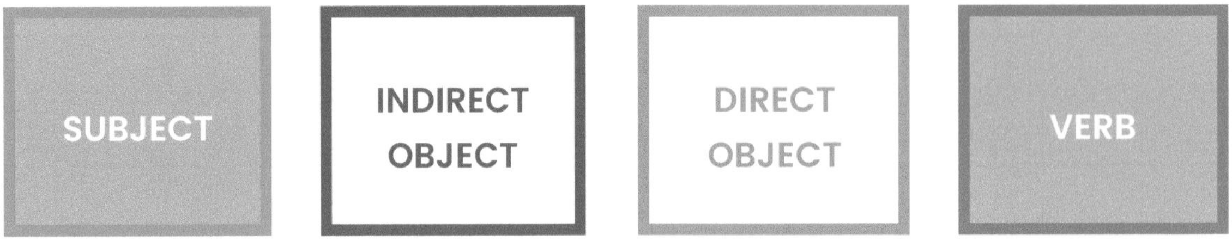

2. Only one thing can interfere: POSTPOSITIONS (A postposition will cancel the gender of the noun before it. As a result, the VERB will agree with the DIRECT OBJECT)

3. If there is no direct object in the sentence, the VERB will assume the default gender of MASCULINE SINGULAR (The indirect object always includes a postposition which cancels its ability to affect gender)

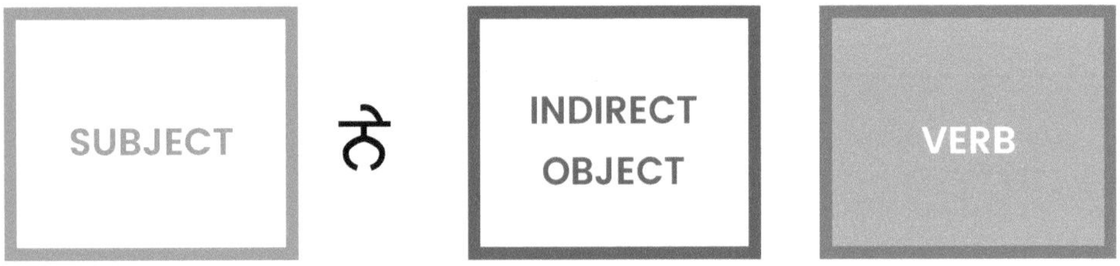

4. Other parts of a sentence with gender include verbals and adjectives.

- VERBALS are in the default gender unless they have an object. (Lesson 4)
- VARIABLE ADJECTIVES agree with the noun they are describing. (Lesson 6)
- POSSESSIVES agree with the object being possessed. (Lesson 6)

DAILY PRACTICE SHEET

Instructions for the 'Think and Speak' method:

Do NOT write down the answers – this is the 'think' part

Say each sentence OUT LOUD – this is the 'speak' part

What if I get stuck? Look at the reference charts for help. The goal is NOT to 'memorize' the sentences but to LEARN A METHOD to construct your own sentences.

SUBJECT + I.OBJECT + D.OBJECT + VERB ROOT + ENDING + AUX.VERB

Exercise One: Verb Roots Ending in Consonants

1. Say each sentence OUT LOUD.
2. Add an indirect OR a direct object and repeat the sentence again. Remember, if you add a direct object, the verb will agree with the direct object.

   For example, "He asked the price" ਉਸ ਨੇ ਕੀਮਤ ਪੁੱਛੀ ਸੀ
3. Add an adjective (e.g. big) or a possessive adjective (e.g. my) to the object. Remember, variable adjectives and possessive adjectives change their endings to reflect the gender and number of the noun that they are describing or possessing.

   For example, "He asked my price" ਉਸ ਨੇ ਮੇਰੀ ਕੀਮਤ ਪੁੱਛੀ ਸੀ

1. He asked.

ਉਸ ਨੇ + ਪੁੱਛ + ending + aux.

= ਉਸ ਨੇ ਪੁੱਛਿਆ ਸੀ

2. We became.
3. They believed/accepted.
4. I changed.
5. She emerged/came out.
6. You found.
7. He asked.
8. We learned.
9. I listened/heard.
10. They met.
11. She opened.
12. You kept.
13. He read.
14. We saw.
15. They touched.
16. I sat.
17. She talked/spoke.
18. You told.
19. He thought.
20. We understood.
21. They walked.
22. I wrote.
23. She bought.
24. You became.
25. He found.

Exercise Two: Irregular Verbs

1. Say each sentence OUT LOUD.

1. She wanted.
ਉਸ ਨੇ + ਚਾਹ + ending + aux.
= ਉਸ ਨੇ ਚਾਹਿਆ ਸੀ
2. We took.
3. They went.
4. You wanted.
5. I had to.
6. She drank.
ਉਸ ਨੇ + ਪੀ + ending + aux.
= ਉਸ ਨੇ ਪੀਤਾ ਸੀ
7. He ate.
8. We slept.
9. They gave.
10. I said.
11. You remained.
12. She did.
13. We drank.
14. They ate.

Exercise Three: Verb Roots Ending in Vowels

1. Say each sentence OUT LOUD.

1. She explained.
ਉਸ ਨੇ + ਸਮਝਾ + ending + aux.
= ਉਸ ਨੇ ਸਮਝਾਇਆ ਸੀ
2. We brought.
3. They called.
4. I came.
5. She drove.
6. You explained.
7. He lost.
8. We made.
9. They saved/rescued.
10. I showed.
11. She sang.
12. You taught.
13. He put on/achieved.

Exercise Four: Habitual Past

1. Say each sentence OUT LOUD.

1. She knew/used to know.
= ਉਹ ਜਾਣਦੀ ਸੀ
2. He use to wish/want.
3. They used to reside.
4. They used to ask.
= ਉਹ ਪੁੱਛਦੇ ਹੁੰਦੇ ਸਨ
5. You used to tell.
6. He used to explain.
7. We used to meet.
8. They used to go.
9. I used to think.
10. You used to teach.

PRACTICE CALENDAR

Box 1: Practice 5 minutes or more of exercise one and then ✓ check box 1

Box 2: Practice 5 minutes or more of exercise two and then ✓ check box 2

Box 3: Practice 5 minutes or more of exercises three & four and then ✓ check box 3

Review Day: Practice lesson five exercises on pages 74-75.

Review Day: Practice lesson four exercises on pages 60-61.

Review Day: Practice lesson three exercises on pages 48-49.

	Week 1			Week 2			Week 3			Week 4		
Monday	1	2	3	1	2	3	1	2	3	1	2	3
Tuesday	1	2	3	1	2	3	1	2	3	1	2	3
Wednesday	1	2	3	1	2	3	1	2	3	1	2	3
Thursday	1	2	3	1	2	3	1	2	3	1	2	3
Friday	1	2	3	1	2	3	1	2	3	1	2	3
Saturday	1	2	3	1	2	3	1	2	3	1	2	3
Sunday	1	2	3	1	2	3	1	2	3	1	2	3

WORKSHEET ANSWERS

Step one: Ask **what is being done?** (Write "V" for verb above the word)
Step two: Ask **who is doing it?** (Write "S" for subject above the word)
Step three: Ask **...what?** (Write "d.O" for direct object above the word)
Step four: Ask **TO what? TO whom?** (Write "i.O" for indirect object above the word)
Step four: Write the English words in the Punjabi word order on the first line
Step five: Write the Punjabi words underneath on the second line.
Step six: Add the appropriate verb ending and auxiliary verb.

1. He read ~~the~~ book.
(present past)

He book read

ਉਸ ਨੇ ਕਿਤਾਬ ਪੜ੍ਹੀ

2. They saw ~~the~~ movie.
(remote past)

They movie saw

ਉਹਨਾਂ ਨੇ ਫਿਲਮ ਦੇਖੀ ਸੀ

3. He used to live in India.
(habitual past)

He India in (used to live)

ਉਹ ਭਾਰਤ ਵਿੱਚ ਰਹਿੰਦਾ ਸੀ

ਉਹ ਭਾਰਤ ਵਿੱਚ ਰਹਿੰਦਾ ਹੁੰਦਾ ਸੀ

4. We wrote ~~a~~ short letter.
(remote past)

We short letter wrote

ਅਸੀਂ ਛੋਟੀ ਚਿੱਠੀ ਲਿਖੀ ਸੀ

5. She told them your name.
(present past)

She them your name told

ਉਸ ਨੇ ਉਹਨਾਂ ਨੂੰ ਤੁਹਾਡਾ ਨਾਮ ਦੱਸਿਆ

Vocabulary: book ਕਿਤਾਬ (feminine) | he/she ਉਹ | in ਵਿੱਚ | India ਭਾਰਤ | letter ਚਿੱਠੀ (feminine) | to live ਰਹਿਣਾ | movie ਫਿਲਮ (feminine) | name ਨਾਮ (masculine) to read ਪੜ੍ਹਨਾ | to see ਦੇਖਣਾ | short ਛੋਟਾ | to tell ਦੱਸਣਾ | they ਉਹ | to ਨੂੰ | was ਸੀ | we ਅਸੀਂ to write ਲਿਖਣਾ | your ਤੁਹਾਡਾ

THE CONTINUOUS TENSE AND QUESTIONS

Continuous Tense

In English, the continuous tense is expressed by adding the ending (ing) to the root of the verb. And it is the auxiliary verb which shows whether the action is past, present or future tense. For example,

"Nick is sending the letter"

"Nick was sending the letter"

"Nick will be sending the letter"

In Punjabi, the continuous tense is expressed by adding the verb ਰਹਿਣਾ *rahiṇā* (to continue) behind the root of the verb. Similar to English, it is the auxiliary verb which shows whether the action is in the present, past or future tense. For example,

ਨਿਕ ਚਿੱਠੀ ਭੇਜ ਰਿਹਾ ਹੈ *Nik ciṭhṭhī bhej rihā hai* (present)

ਨਿਕ ਚਿੱਠੀ ਭੇਜ ਰਿਹਾ ਸੀ *Nik ciṭhṭhī bhej rihā sī* (past)

ਨਿਕ ਚਿੱਠੀ ਭੇਜ ਰਿਹਾ ਹੋਵੇਗਾ *Nik ciṭhṭhī bhej rihā hovegā* (future)

Notice in the examples above, the verb ਰਿਹਾ *rihā* (which is the past tense form of the verb ਰਹਿਣਾ *rahiṇā*) is not attached to the stem. Both ਰਿਹਾ *rihā* and the auxiliary verb change according to the number and gender of the subject.

ਰਿਹਾ *rihā* (masculine singular) ਰਹੀ *rahī* (feminine singular)

ਰਹੇ *rahe* (masculine plural) ਰਹੀਆਂ *rahīā̃* (feminine plural)

For example: "We are sending a letter."

SUBJECT	DIRECT OBJECT	VERB + AUX.VERB
We	letter	send-ing are
ਅਸੀਂ	ਚਿੱਠੀ	ਭੇਜ ਰਹੇ ਹਾਂ
āsīṇ	*ciṭhṭhī*	*bhej rahe hāṇ*

To make a negative sentence, simply insert the word ਨਹੀ *nahīṇ* (not) before the main verb. For example: "Nick is not sending a letter."

SUBJECT	DIRECT OBJECT	VERB + AUX.VERB
Nick	letter	not send-ing is
ਨਿਕ	ਚਿੱਠੀ	ਨਹੀਂ ਭੇਜ ਰਿਹਾ ਹੈ
Nik	*ciṭhṭhī*	*nahīṇ bhej rihā hai*

Go ahead and complete sentences 1 and 2 on the worksheet on page 103.

Conjunct Verbs

In English some words can be used as both nouns and verbs. For example, in the sentence "They answer" the word 'answer' is the verb. However, in the sentence "They want an answer" the word 'answer' is the object. So 'answer' can be used as a noun or a verb.

In Punjabi, a noun (or adjective) can ONLY be used as a verb if it is joined with a base verb. This is called a conjunct verb. Conjunct means something that is joined with another. The noun (or adjective) is joined with a base verb. The base verb loses its primary meaning to take on the meaning of the noun (or adjective).

For example, "They answer." (lit. "They give an answer")

SUBJECT	DIRECT OBJECT	VERB + AUX.VERB
They	answer	~~give~~ are
ਉਹ	ਜਵਾਬ	ਦਿੰਦੇ ਹਨ
uh	*javāb*	*diṇde han*

In the next sentence, notice that ਨਹੀਂ *nahīṇ* is still inserted before the base verb. For example: "They ~~do~~ not answer." (lit. "They do not give an answer")

SUBJECT	DIRECT OBJECT	VERB + AUX.VERB
They	answer	not ~~give~~ are
ਉਹ	ਜਵਾਬ	ਨਹੀਂ ਦਿੰਦੇ ਹਨ
uh	*javāb*	*nahīṇ diṇde han*

When a direct object is used with the conjunct verb, the position word ਦਾ *dā* is normally added between the two objects. For example, "They answer ~~the~~ question" (lit. "They give the answer of the question")

SUBJECT	DIRECT OBJECT	VERB + AUX.VERB
They	question of answer	~~give~~ are
ਉਹ	ਸਵਾਲ ਦਾ ਜਵਾਬ	ਦਿੰਦੇ ਹਨ
uh	*savāl dā javāb*	*diṇde han*

The position word ਦਾ *dā* takes the gender of the conjunct verb. In this case, the word 'answer' is masculine singular. Go ahead and complete sentence 3.

When a verbal is used with the conjunct verb, the position word ਦਾ *dā* is also normally added between the two objects. Again, the position word ਦਾ *dā* takes the gender of the conjunct verb. Notice in the sentence below, the verbal is followed by a position word and uses the oblique spelling. "They decide to go" (lit. "They do the decision of going.")

SUBJECT	DIRECT OBJECT	VERB + AUX.VERB
They	to go of decision	~~do~~ are
ਉਹ	ਜਾਣ ਦਾ ਫ਼ੈਸਲਾ	ਕਰਦੇ ਹਨ
uh	*jāṇ dā faislā*	*karde han*

When an indirect object is added to the sentence, the choice of the position word is determined not only by the context but also by the conjunct verb being used.
For example, with the conjunct verb "to help" ਮਦਦ ਕਰਨੀ *madad karnī* the position word 'of' ਦਾ *dā* is normally used with the indirect object. For example, "They help him." (lit. "They do his help")

SUBJECT	INDIRECT OBJECT	DIRECT OBJECT	VERB + AUX.VERB
They	him	help	~~do~~ are
ਉਹ	ਉਸ ਦੀ	ਮਦਦ	ਕਰਦੇ ਹਨ
uh	*us dī*	*madad*	*karde han*

Notice in the sentence above, that the possessive adjective ਦਾ *dā* changes according to the object being possessed (the conjunct verb 'help') and not according to the possessor.

In the next sentence, you will notice that when the gender of the subject is canceled by a position word, the base verb takes the gender of the conjunct verb.

For example, in the sentence "They helped him" the conjunct verb 'help' is feminine singular.

SUBJECT	INDIRECT OBJECT	DIRECT OBJECT	VERB + AUX.VERB
They	him	helped	~~did~~ was
ਉਹਨਾਂ ਨੇ	ਉਸ ਦੀ	ਮਦਦ	ਕੀਤੀ ਸੀ
uhnāṇ ne	*us dī*	*madad*	*kītī sī*

The verb 'to do' ਕਰਨਾ *karnā* is most commonly used in conjunct verbs, however, other verbs are also used. Remember, when using the verb "to do" ਕਰਨਾ *karnā* in the past tense, it has an irregular spelling ਕੀਤਾ *kītā*

Asking Questions

Interrogatives are words used in asking questions. In Punjabi, most interrogative words begin with the letter ਕ *k* for example: who ਕੌਣ *kauṇ*, what ਕੀ *kī*, where ਕਿੱਥੇ *kiththe*, when ਕਦੋਂ *kadoṇ*, why ਕਿਉਂ *kiuṇ*, which ਕਿਹੜਾ *kihṛā*, how ਕਿਵੇਂ *kiveṇ*, & how much ਕਿੰਨਾ *kiṇnā*

Where to put interrogatives in the sentence depends upon the context. As a guideline, you can ask these questions:

1. Am I asking about an action? Then the interrogative goes before the verb. e.g. "When will I read the magazine?"

SUBJECT	DIRECT OBJECT	VERB + AUX.VERB
I	magazine	**when** will read?
ਮੈਂ	ਰਸਾਲਾ	ਕਦੋਂ ਪੜ੍ਹਾਂਗਾ?
maiṇ	*rasālā*	*kadoṇ paṛrāṇgā?*

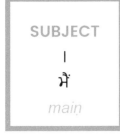

2. Am I asking about an object? Then the interrogative goes before the object. e.g. "Which magazine will I read?"

SUBJECT	DIRECT OBJECT	VERB + AUX.VERB
I	**which** magazine	will read?
ਮੈਂ	ਕਿਹੜਾ ਰਸਾਲਾ	ਪੜ੍ਹਾਂਗਾ?
maiṇ	*kihṛā rasālā*	*paṛrāṇgā?*

TIP: The easiest way to form a question is to first form a statement. Then it is easy to add in the interrogative. For example: "Where will he go?"

First: Form a statement. "He will go"

Second: Insert the interrogative. "He ^ will go"

where

Both ਕਿਹੜਾ and ਕਿੰਨਾ are variable and change according to the gender and number of the noun to which they are referring. For example: "Which letter will Nick send?"

SUBJECT	DIRECT OBJECT	VERB + AUX.VERB
Nick	**which** letter	will send ?
ਨਿਕ	ਕਿਹੜੀ ਚਿੱਠੀ	ਭੇਜੇਗਾ?
Nik	*kihṛī ciṭhṭhī*	*bhejegā?*

TIP: ਕੌਣ *kauṇ* (who) and ਕੀ *kī* (what) are interrogative pronouns and change when followed by a position word. For example, in English, the oblique spelling of 'who' is 'whom.' Similarly, in Punjabi ਕੌਣ *kauṇ* and ਕੀ *kī* change to ਕਿਸ *kis* when followed by a postposition. For example: "You wrote to whom?" ਤੁਸੀਂ ਕਿਸ ਨੂੰ ਲਿਖਿਆ ਸੀ? *tusīṇ kis nūṇ likhiā sī?* Go ahead and complete sentence 4 on the worksheet.

Yes or No Questions

When ਕੀ *kī* is at the beginning of a sentence, its meaning changes. Now its function is to turn statements into questions, the type of questions which are answered with a yes or no reply. For example: "Nick sends letters"

SUBJECT	DIRECT OBJECT	VERB + AUX.VERB
Nick	letters	sends is
ਨਿਕ	ਚਿੱਠੀਆਂ	ਭੇਜਦਾ ਹੈ
Nik	*ciṭhṭhīāṇ*	*bhejdā hai*

Becomes: "Does Nick send letters?"

SUBJECT	DIRECT OBJECT	VERB + AUX.VERB
Does Nick	letters	send is?
ਕੀ ਨਿਕ	ਚਿੱਠੀਆਂ	ਭੇਜਦਾ ਹੈ?
kī Nik	*ciṭhṭhīāṇ*	*bhejdā hai?*

Go ahead and complete sentence 5 on the worksheet.

What time is it?

In lesson five we learned how to say "It is two o'clock" ਦੋ ਵਜੇ ਹਨ *do vaje han* (lit. two chimes are) Now we can turn that statement into a question. We can ask: 'how many chimes?' ਕਿੰਨੇ ਵਜੇ ਹਨ? *kiṇne vaje han?*

This informal way to ask the time can also be adapted to more formal situations.

For example, “Can you tell me the time?”

SUBJECT	I.OJECT	VERB + AUX.		SUBJECT	AUX.
Can you	me	tell ~~can~~ is	that	how many chimes	are?
ਕੀ ਤੁਸੀਂ	ਮੈਨੂੰ	ਦੱਸ ਸਕਦੇ ਹੋ	ਕਿ	ਕਿੰਨੇ ਵਜੇ	ਹਨ?
kī tusīṇ	*mainūṇ*	*dass sakde ho*	*ki*	*kiṇne vaje*	*han?*

Notice in the above sentence that adding ਕੀ *kī* to the beginning of the first sentence turns the statement “You can tell me the time” into a question “Can you tell me the time?” So we see that ਕੀ *kī* can take on different meanings depending on the sentence. However, it will always turn a statement into the type of question that can be answered with a yes or no reply.

The daily practice sheet in this lesson contains four exercises. We will divide the fifteen minutes of practice between these four exercises. It is important to spend at least a few minutes on each exercise.

The practice calendar continues to use a rotating practice schedule. When you feel comfortable with performing the exercises then you have completed the course. Congratulations! The charts and information contained in the course will continue to be a valuable source of reference for you as you progress in your language skills.

LESSON SEVEN WORKSHEET

Step one: Ask **what is being done?** (Write "V" for verb above the word)
Step two: Ask **who is doing it?** (Write "S" for subject above the word)
Step three: Ask **...what?** (Write "d.O" for direct object above the word)
Step four: Ask **TO what? TO whom?** (Write "i.O" for indirect object above the word)
Step four: Write the English words in the Punjabi word order on the first line
Step five: Write the Punjabi words underneath on the second line.
Step six: Add the appropriate verb ending and auxiliary verb.

1. I am eating roti. ______________________________

____

2. He will be going. ______________________________

____

3. They enjoy a meal. ______________________________

____

4. How do we know? ______________________________

____

5. Do you speak Punjabi? ______________________________

____

Vocabulary: am ਹਾਂ | are ਹਨ / ਹੋ | to eat ਖਾਣਾ | to enjoy ਆਨੰਦ ਮਾਣਨਾ | to go ਜਾਣਾ
he ਉਹ | how ਕਿਵੇਂ | I ਮੈਂ | is ਹੈ | to know ਜਾਣਨਾ | meal ਖਾਣਾ (masc.) | Punjabi ਪੰਜਾਬੀ
roti ਰੋਟੀ (feminine) | to speak ਬੋਲਣਾ | they ਉਹ | we ਅਸੀਂ | what ਕੀ | you ਤੁਸੀਂ

DAILY PRACTICE SHEET VOCABULARY

to answer ਜਵਾਬ ਦੇਣਾ *javāb deṇā*	to appreciate ਕਦਰ ਕਰਨੀ *kadar karnī*	to begin/start ਸ਼ੁਰੂ ਕਰਨਾ *shurū karnā*
to decide ਫ਼ੈਸਲਾ ਕਰਨਾ *faislā karnā*	to enjoy ਆਨੰਦ ਮਾਣਨਾ *ānaṇd māṇnā*	to finish ਖ਼ਤਮ ਕਰਨਾ *khatam karnā*
to help ਮਦਦ ਕਰਨੀ *madad karnī*	how ਕਿਵੇਂ *kiveṇ*	how much/many ਕਿੰਨਾ *kiṇnā*
to love ਪਿਆਰ ਕਰਨਾ *piār karnā*	to promise ਵਾਅਦਾ ਕਰਨਾ *vādā karnā*	to remember ਯਾਦ ਰੱਖਣੀ *yād rakhkhaṇī*
to remind ਯਾਦ ਕਰਾਉਣੀ *yād karāuṇī*	to try ਕੋਸ਼ਿਸ਼ ਕਰਨੀ *koshish karnī*	what ਕੀ *kī*
when ਕਦੋਂ *kadoṇ*	where ਕਿਥੇ *kithe*	which ਕਿਹੜਾ *kihṛā*
who ਕੌਣ *kauṇ*	why ਕਿਉਂ *kiuṇ*	to work ਕੰਮ ਕਰਨਾ *kaṇm karnā*

DAILY PRACTICE SHEET

Instructions for the 'Think and Speak' method:

Do NOT write down the answers – this is the 'think' part

Say each sentence OUT LOUD – this is the 'speak' part

What if I get stuck? Look at the reference charts for help. The goal is NOT to 'memorize' the sentences but to LEARN A METHOD to construct your own sentences.

Exercise One: Present Continuous Tense

1. Say each sentence OUT LOUD.

1. He is asking.
= ਉਹ ਪੁੱਛ ਰਿਹਾ ਹੈ
2. We are changing.
3. They are learning.
4. I am taking.
5. She is reading.
6. You are making.
7. We are meeting.
8. He is coming.

Exercise Two: Past Continuous Tense

1. Say each sentence OUT LOUD.

1. She was living/residing.
= ਉਹ ਰਹਿ ਰਿਹੀ ਸੀ
2. We were drinking.
3. They were sleeping.
4. I was listening.
5. She was eating.
6. You were thinking.
7. He was doing.
8. I was bringing.

Exercise Three: Future Continuous Tense

1. Say each sentence OUT LOUD.

1. We will be explaining.
= ਅਸੀਂ ਸਮਝਾ ਰਿਹੇ ਹੋਵਾਂਗੇ
2. He will be showing.
3. They will be singing.
4. I will be going.
5. She will be telling.
6. We will be talking.
7. He will be achieving.
8. You will be giving.

Exercise Four: Conjunct Verbs

1. Say each sentence OUT LOUD.
2. Add an indirect OR a direct object (including verbals) and repeat the sentence again.

1. He works.
= ਉਹ ਕੰਮ ਕਰਦਾ ਹੈ
2. We answer.
3. They appreciate.
4. I begin/start.
5. She decides.
6. You enjoy.
7. He finishes.
8. We help.
9. They love.
10. I promise.
11. You remember.
12. She reminds.
13. We try.
14. They work.

Exercise Five: Questions

1. Say each sentence OUT LOUD.

1. Where is the house?
= ਘਰ ਕਿੱਥੇ ਹੈ?
2. When will you come?
3. Where does she reside?
4. How can we learn?
5. He meets with whom?
6. Which book do you read?
7. I speak to whom?
8. What will we eat?
9. Who will go?
10. What do they see?
11. How do we ask?

Exercise Six: Yes or No Questions

1. Say each sentence OUT LOUD.

1. Does he work?
= ਕੀ ਉਹ ਕੰਮ ਕਰਦਾ ਹੈ?
2. Can we explain?
3. Do they see?
4. Will I understand?
5. Did you eat?
6. Can she speak?
7. Does he want to go?
8. Will we walk?
9. Did they sing?
10. Can I read?
11. Do you know?

PRACTICE CALENDAR

Box 1: Practice 5 minutes or more of exercises one to three and then ✓ check box 1

Box 2: Practice 5 minutes or more of exercise four and then ✓ check box 2

Box 3: Practice 5 minutes or more of exercises five & six and then ✓ check box 3

Review Day: Practice lesson six exercises on pages 91-92.

Review Day: Practice lesson five exercises on pages 74-75.

Review Day: Practice lesson four exercises on pages 60-61.

Review Day: Practice lesson three exercises on pages 48-49.

	Week 1			Week 2			Week 3			Week 4		
Monday	1	2	3	1	2	3	1	2	3	1	2	3
Tuesday	1	2	3	1	2	3	1	2	3	1	2	3
Wednesday	1	2	3	1	2	3	1	2	3	1	2	3
Thursday	1	2	3	1	2	3	1	2	3	1	2	3
Friday	1	2	3	1	2	3	1	2	3	1	2	3
Saturday	1	2	3	1	2	3	1	2	3	1	2	3
Sunday	1	2	3	1	2	3	1	2	3	1	2	3

WORKSHEET ANSWERS

Step one: Ask **what is being done?** (Write "V" for verb above the word)
Step two: Ask **who is doing it?** (Write "S" for subject above the word)
Step three: Ask **...what?** (Write "d.O" for direct object above the word)
Step four: Ask **TO what? TO whom?** (Write "i.O" for indirect object above the word)
Step four: Write the English words in the Punjabi word order on the first line
Step five: Write the Punjabi words underneath on the second line.
Step six: Add the appropriate verb ending and auxiliary verb.

1. I am eating roti.

I roti eat-ing am

ਮੈਂ ਰੋਟੀ ਖਾ ਰਿਹਾ ਹਾਂ (masculine)
ਮੈਂ ਰੋਟੀ ਖਾ ਰਿਹੀ ਹਾਂ (feminine)

2. He will be going.

He go-ing will be

ਉਹ ਜਾ ਰਿਹਾ ਹੋਵੇਗਾ

3. They enjoy ~~a~~ meal.

They meal enjoy

ਉਹ ਖਾਣੇ ਦਾ ਆਨੰਦ ਮਾਣਦੇ ਹਨ

4. How ~~do~~ we know?

We how know

ਅਸੀਂ ਕਿਵੇਂ ਜਾਣਦੇ ਹਾਂ ?

5. Do you speak Punjabi?

Do you Punjabi speak

ਕੀ ਤੁਸੀਂ ਪੰਜਾਬੀ ਬੋਲਦੇ ਹੋ ?

Vocabulary: am ਹਾਂ | are ਹਨ / ਹੋ | to eat ਖਾਣਾ | to enjoy ਆਨੰਦ ਮਾਣਨਾ | to go ਜਾਣਾ
he ਉਹ | how ਕਿਵੇਂ | I ਮੈਂ | is ਹੈ | to know ਜਾਣਨਾ | meal ਖਾਣਾ (masc.) | Punjabi ਪੰਜਾਬੀ
roti ਰੋਟੀ (feminine) | to speak ਬੋਲਣਾ | they ਉਹ | we ਅਸੀਂ | what ਕੀ | you ਤੁਸੀਂ

Index

CPSIA information can be obtained
at www.ICGtesting.com
Printed in the USA
LVHW072231020423
743290LV00014B/68

9780998482804